Lupita Romo
Easy Flower Mandalas

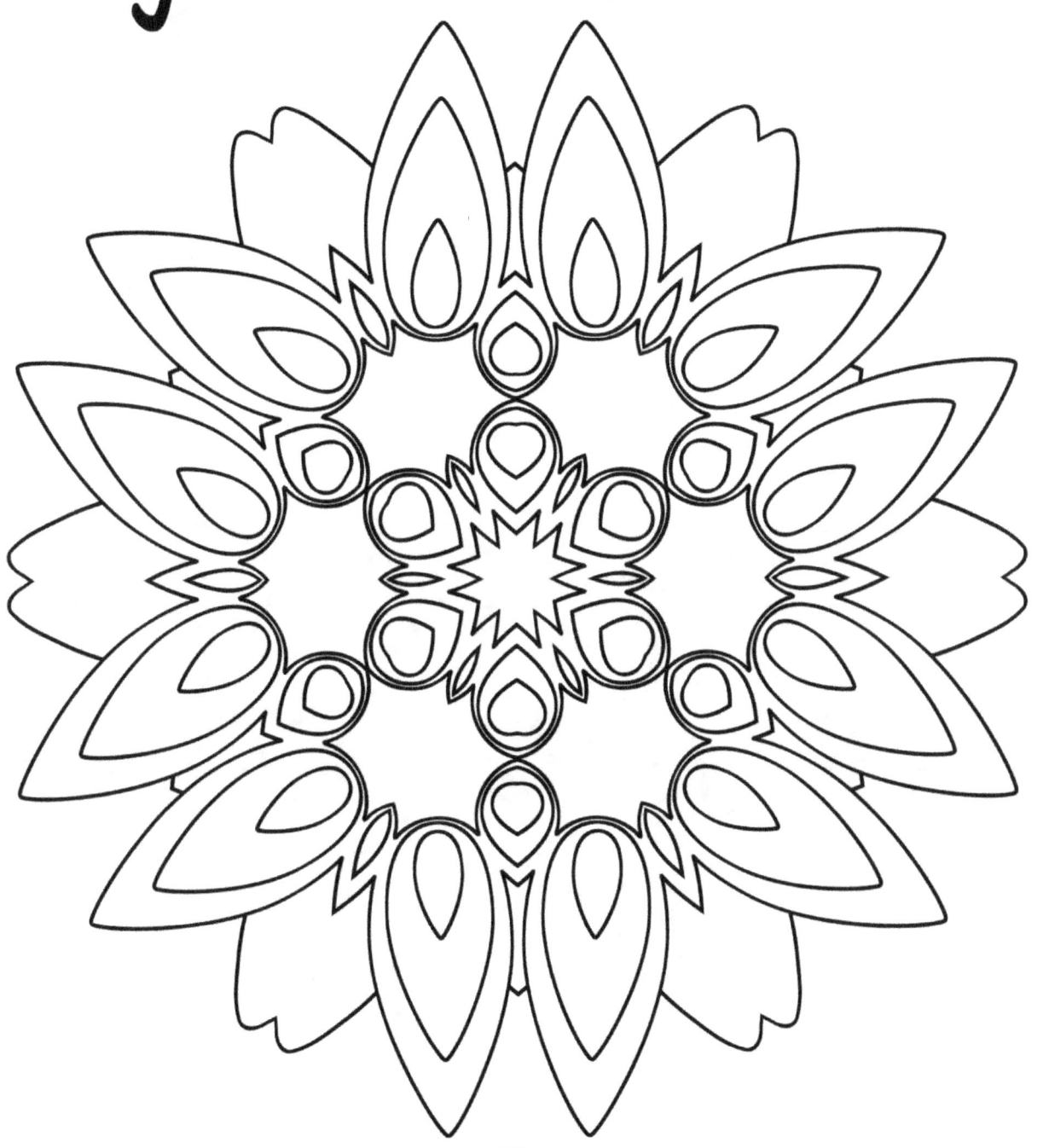

Adults Coloring Book
For beginners, seniors and individuals with low vision

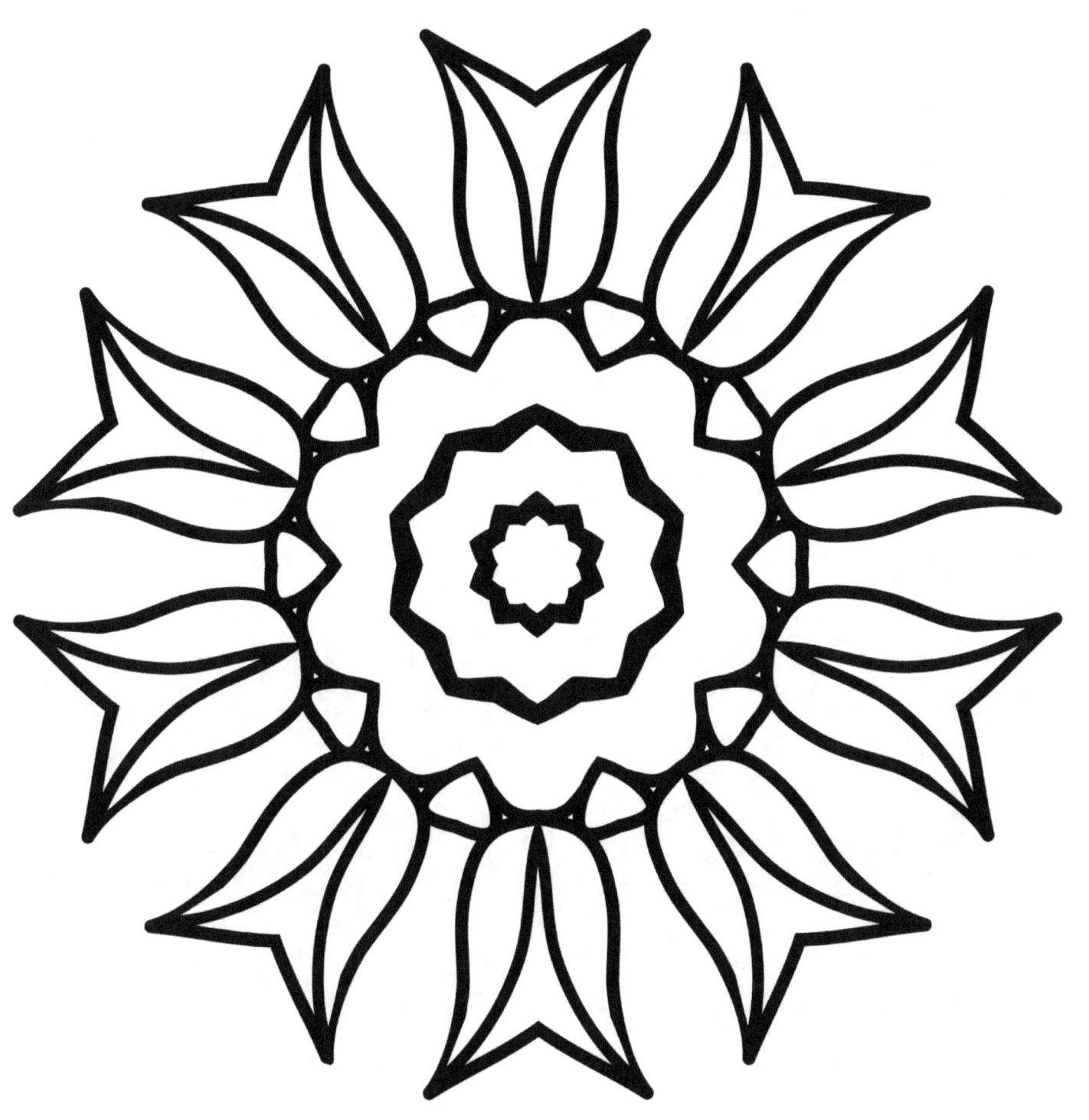

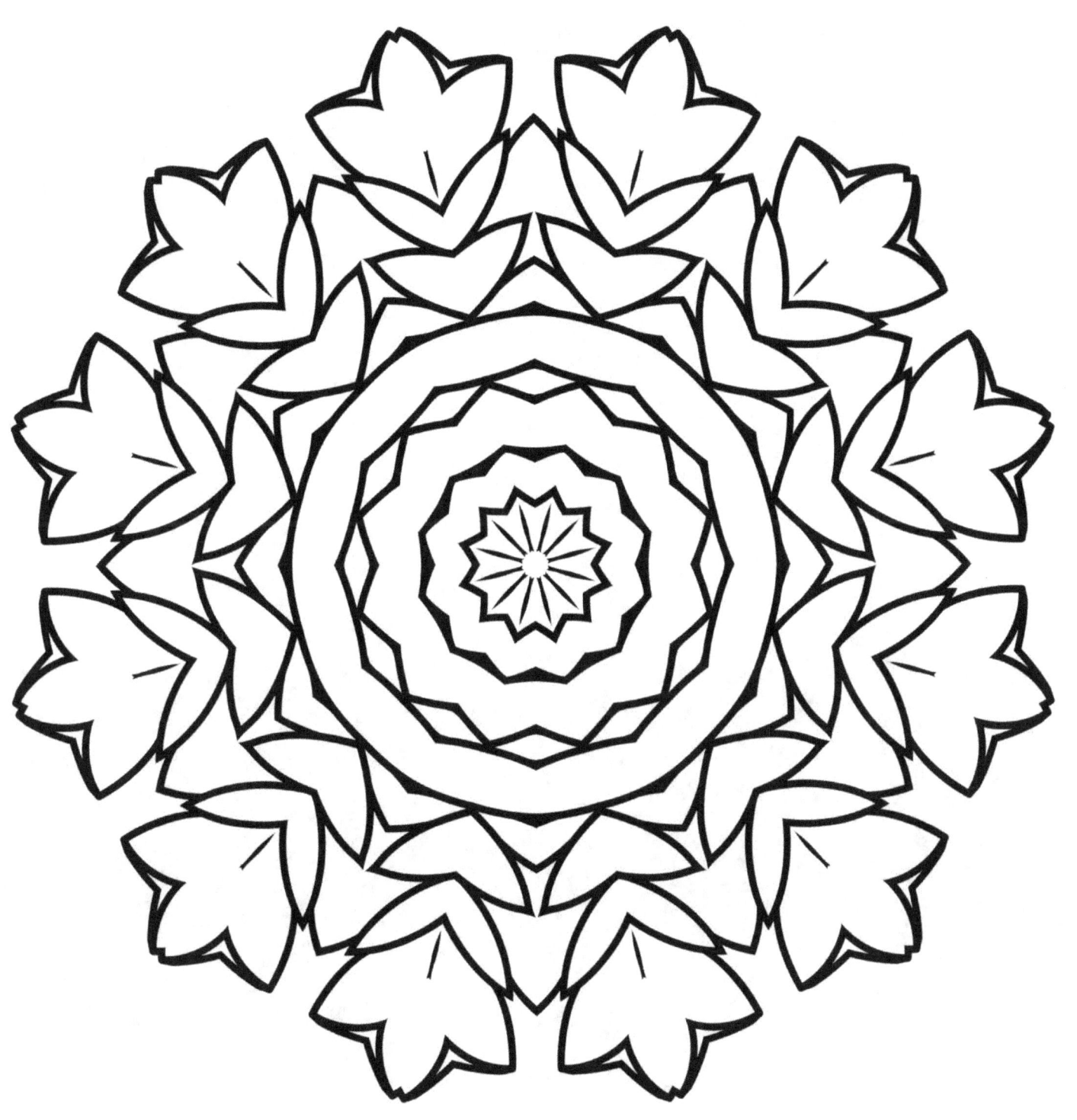

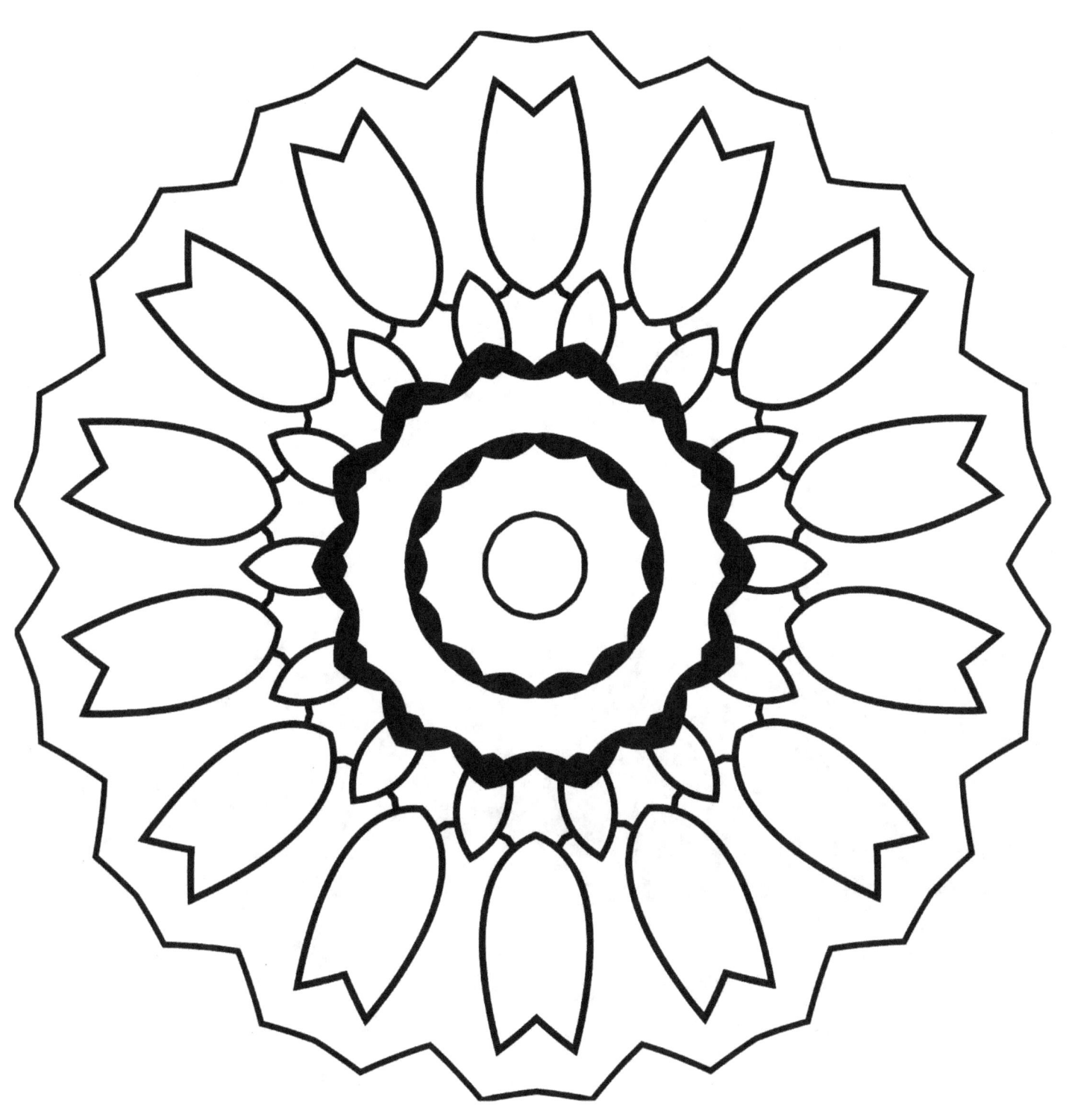

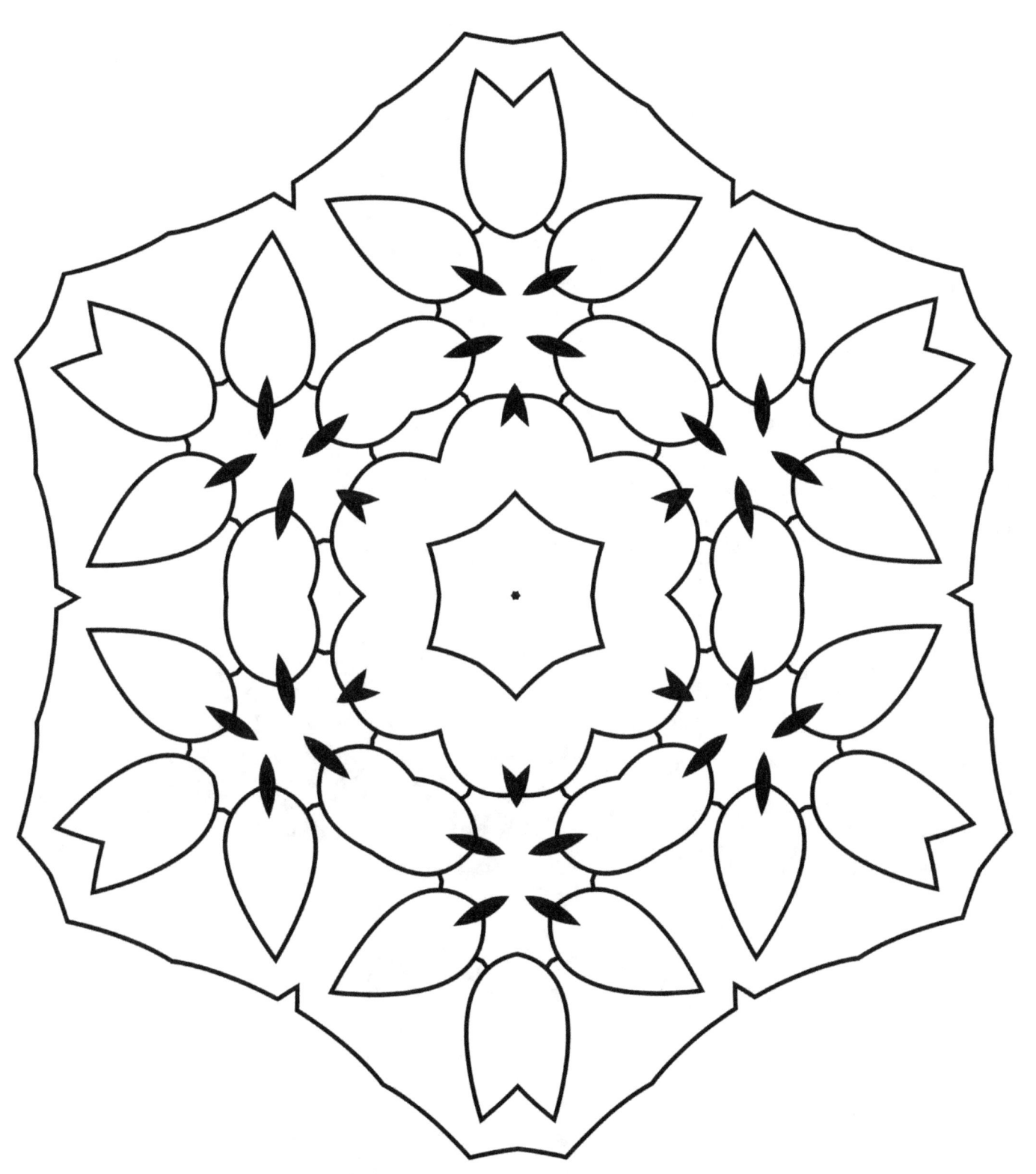

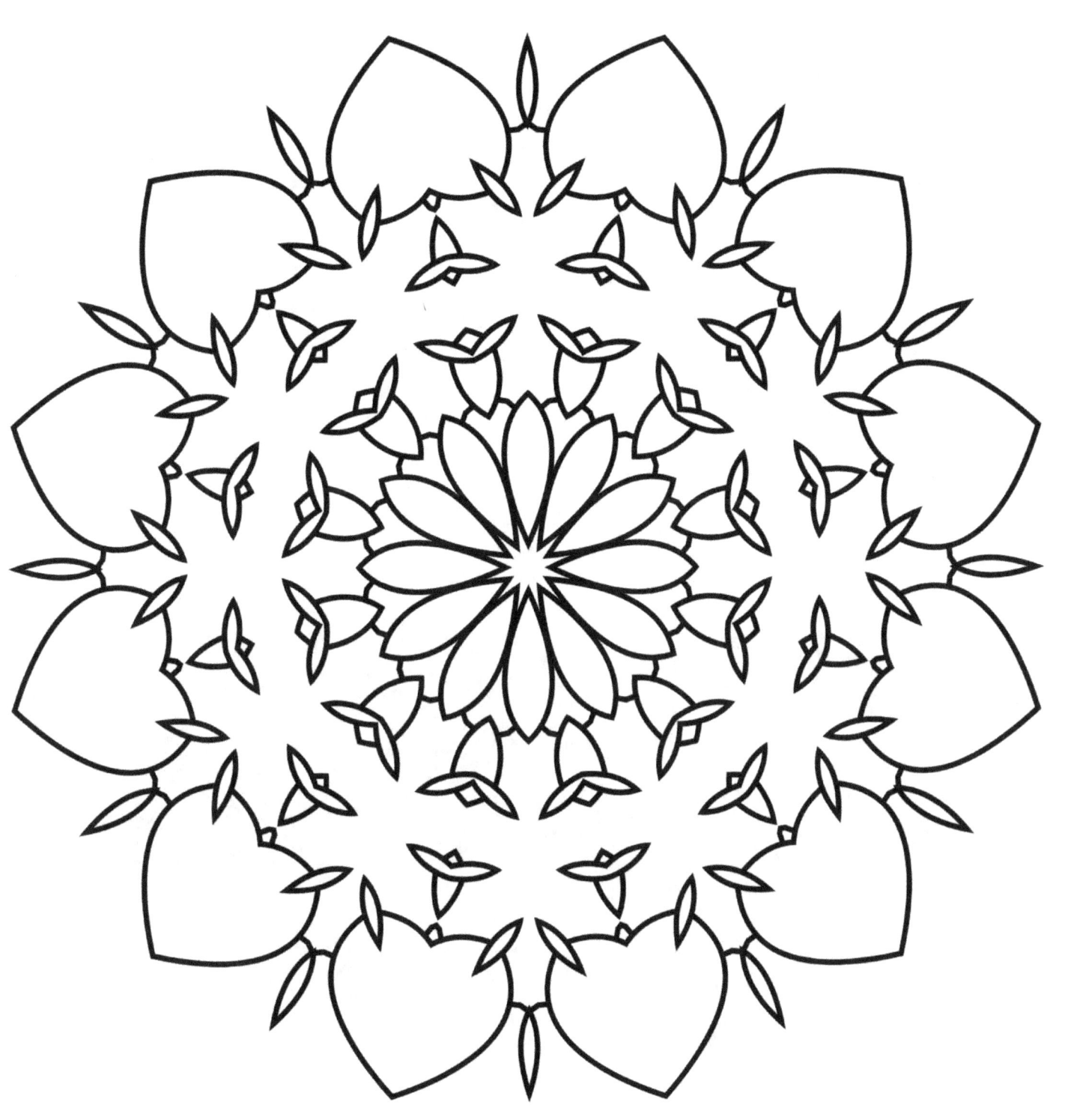

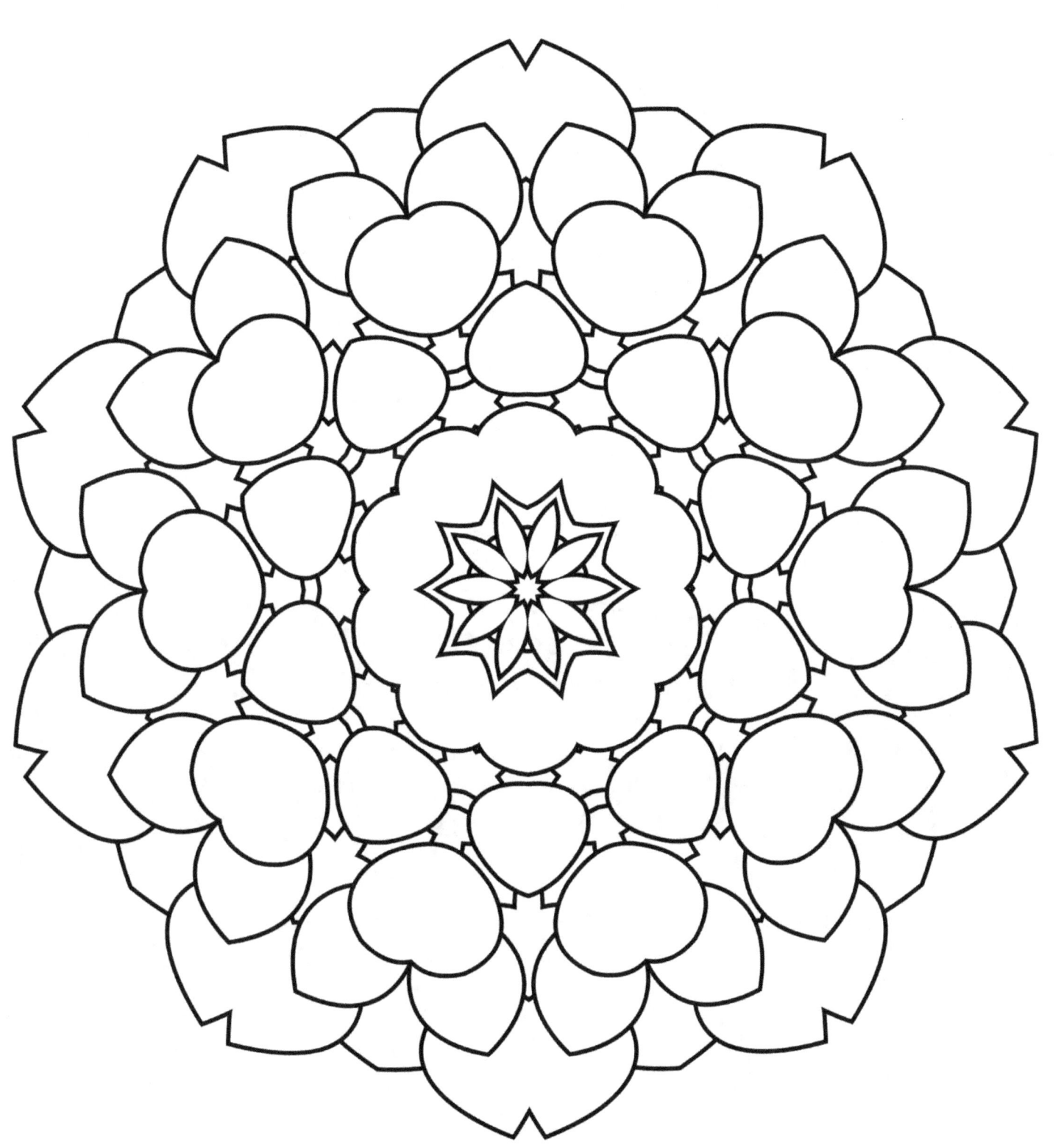

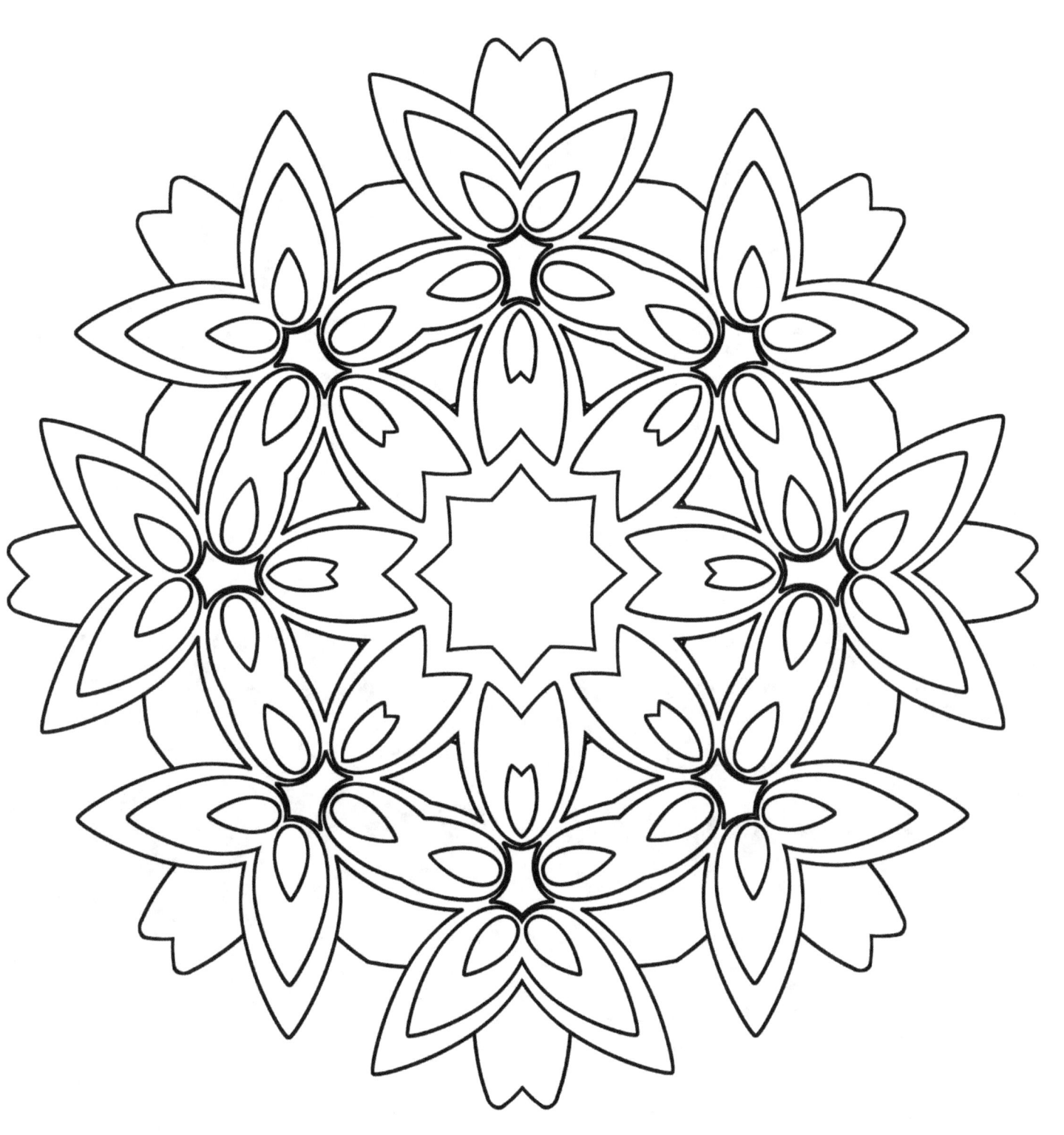

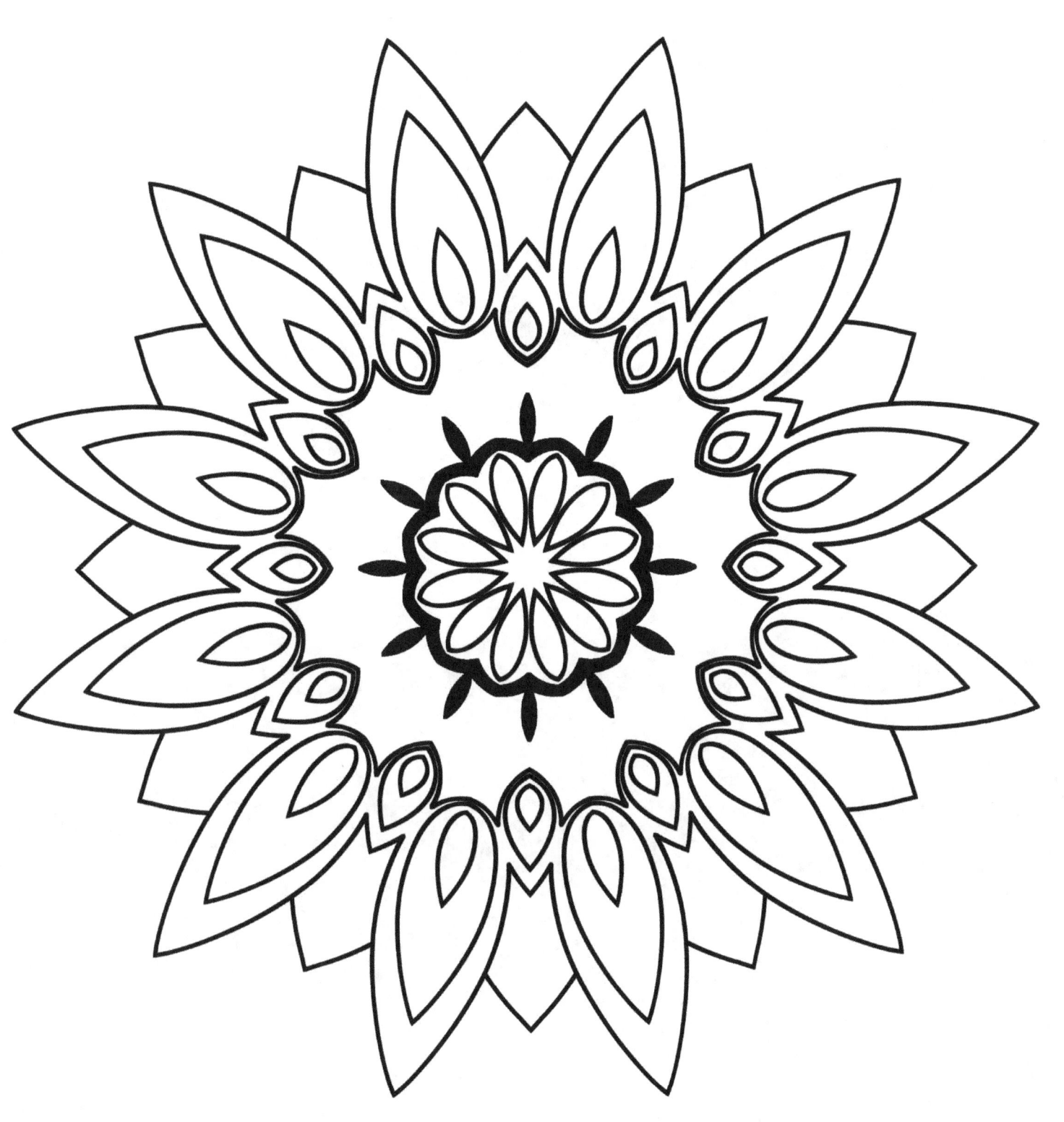

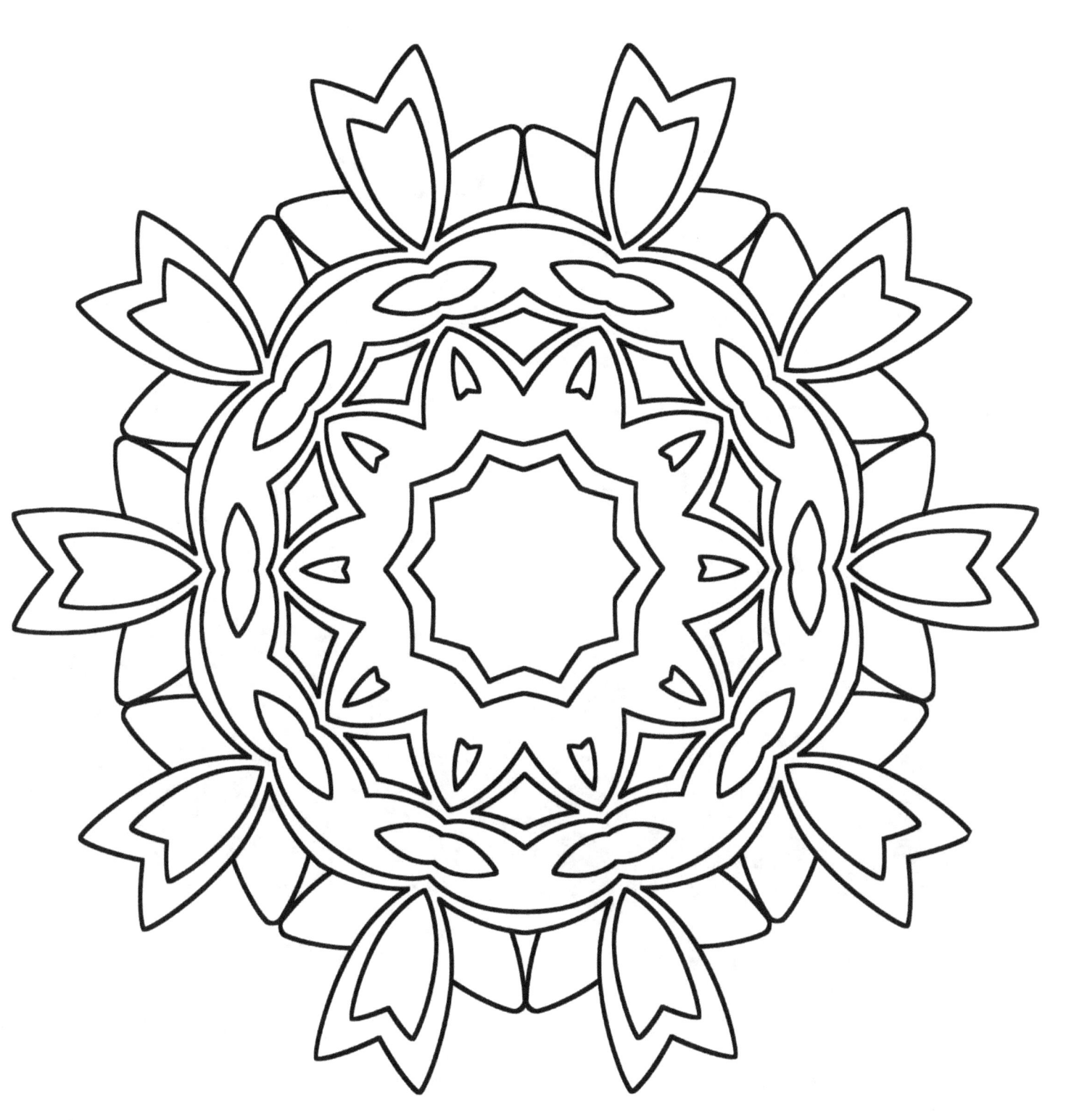

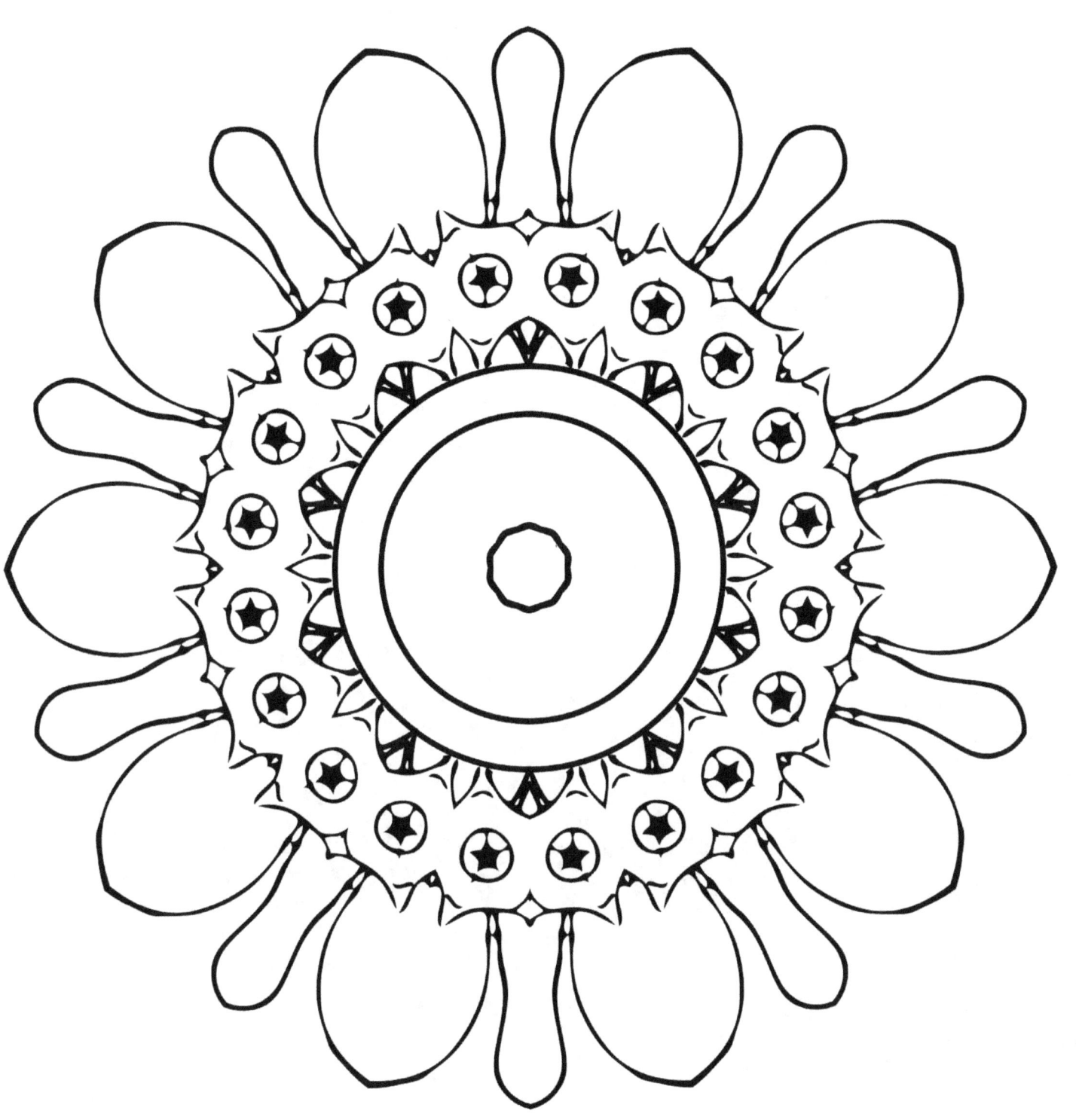

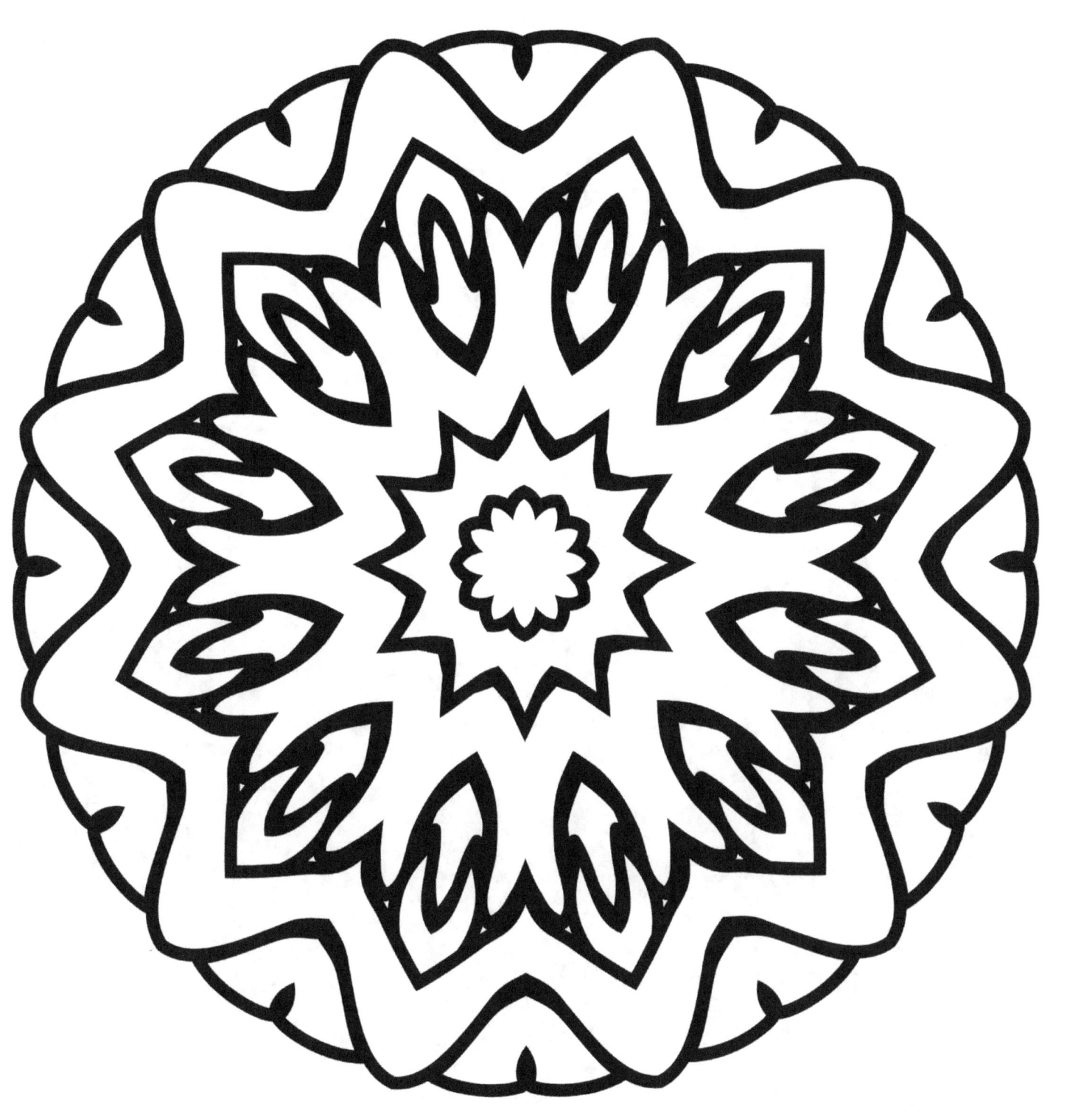

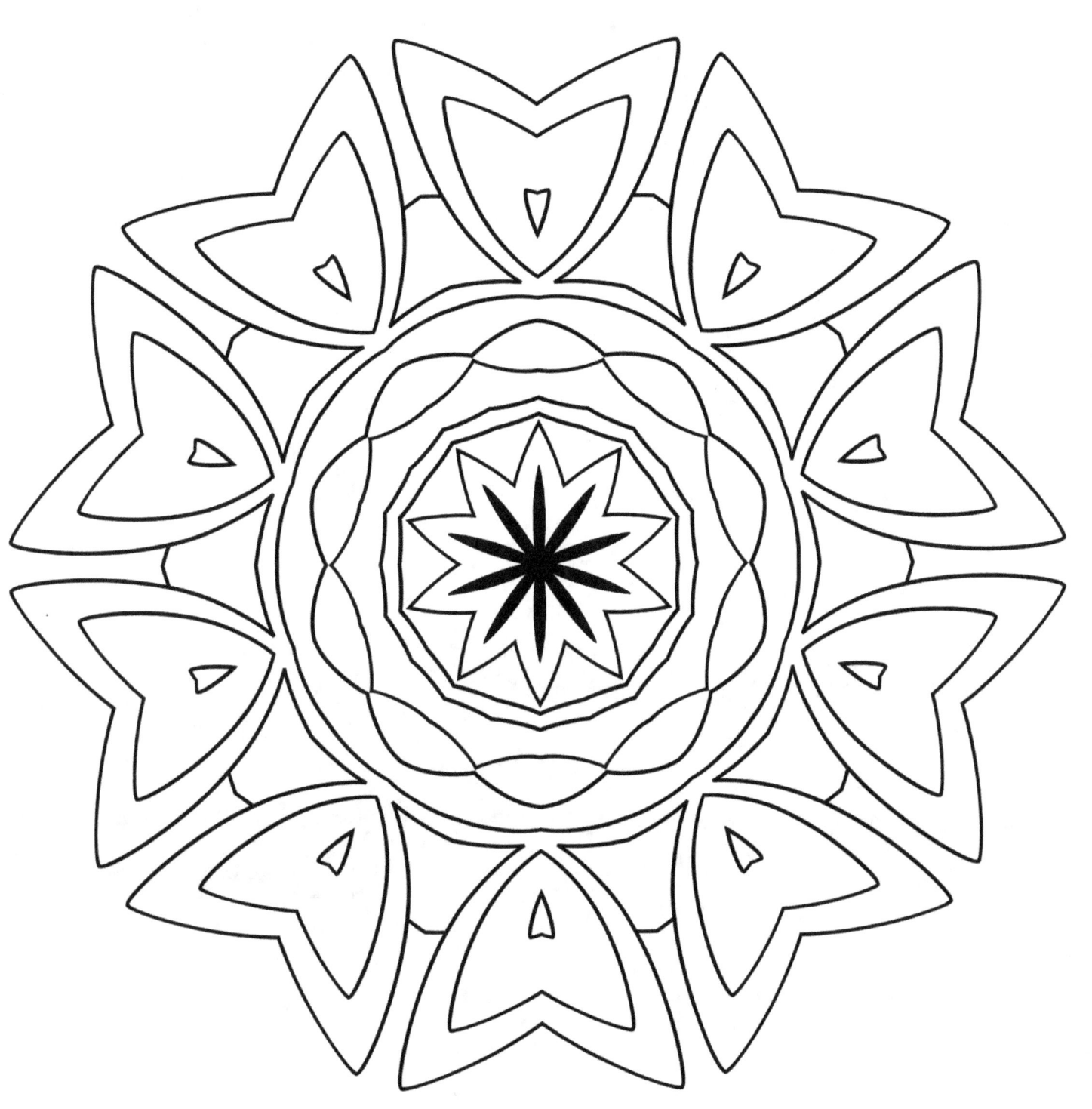

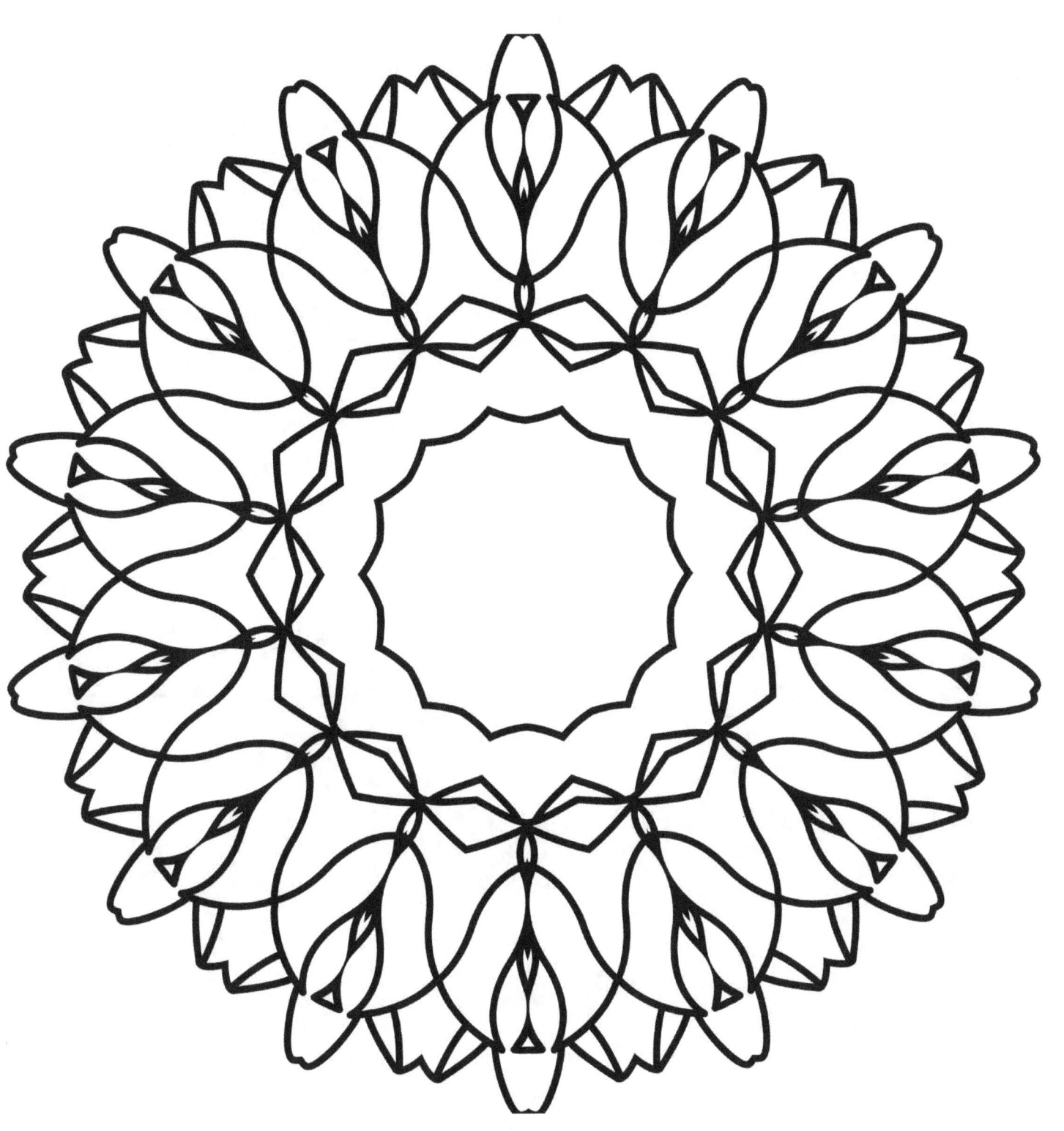

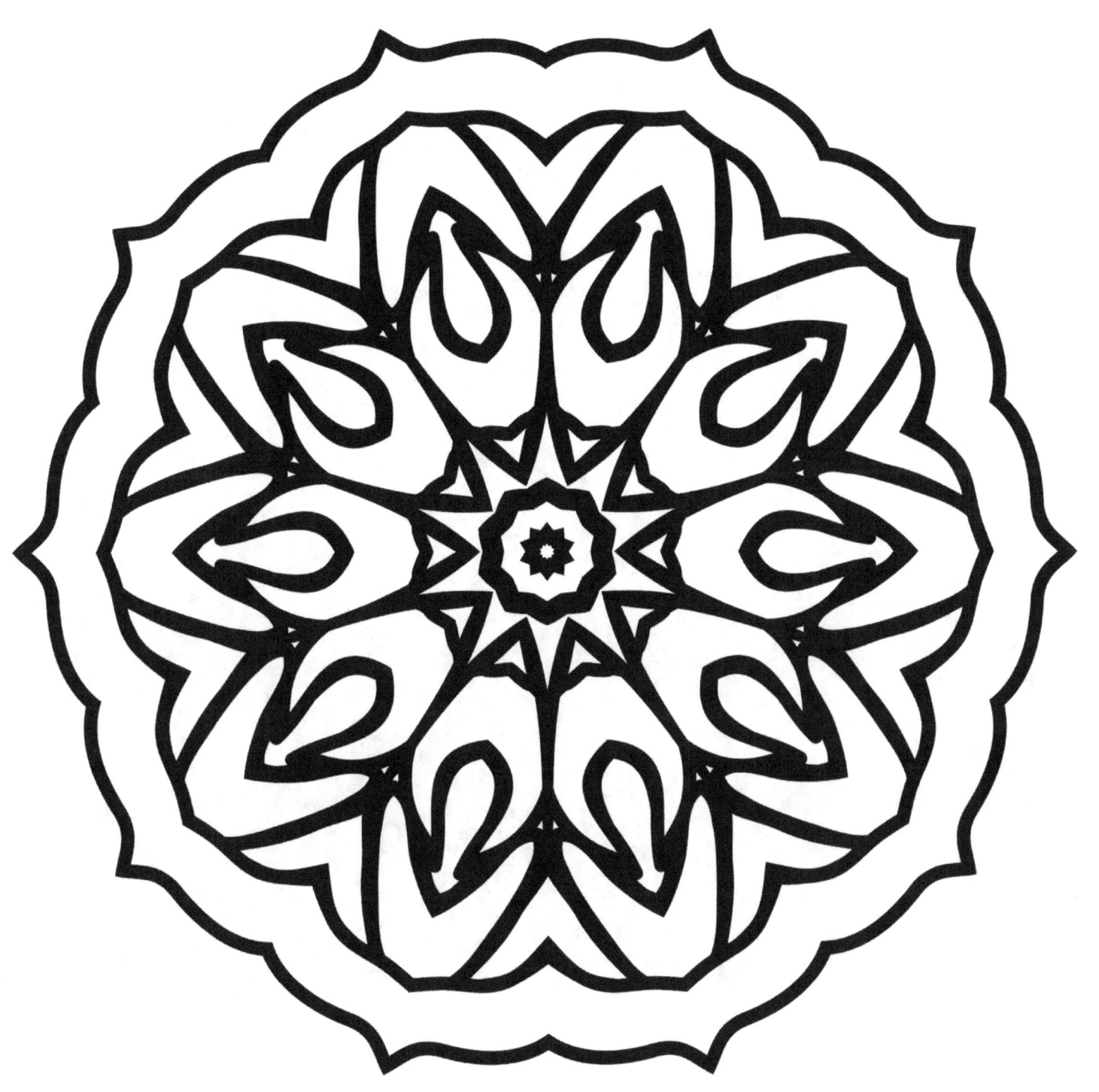

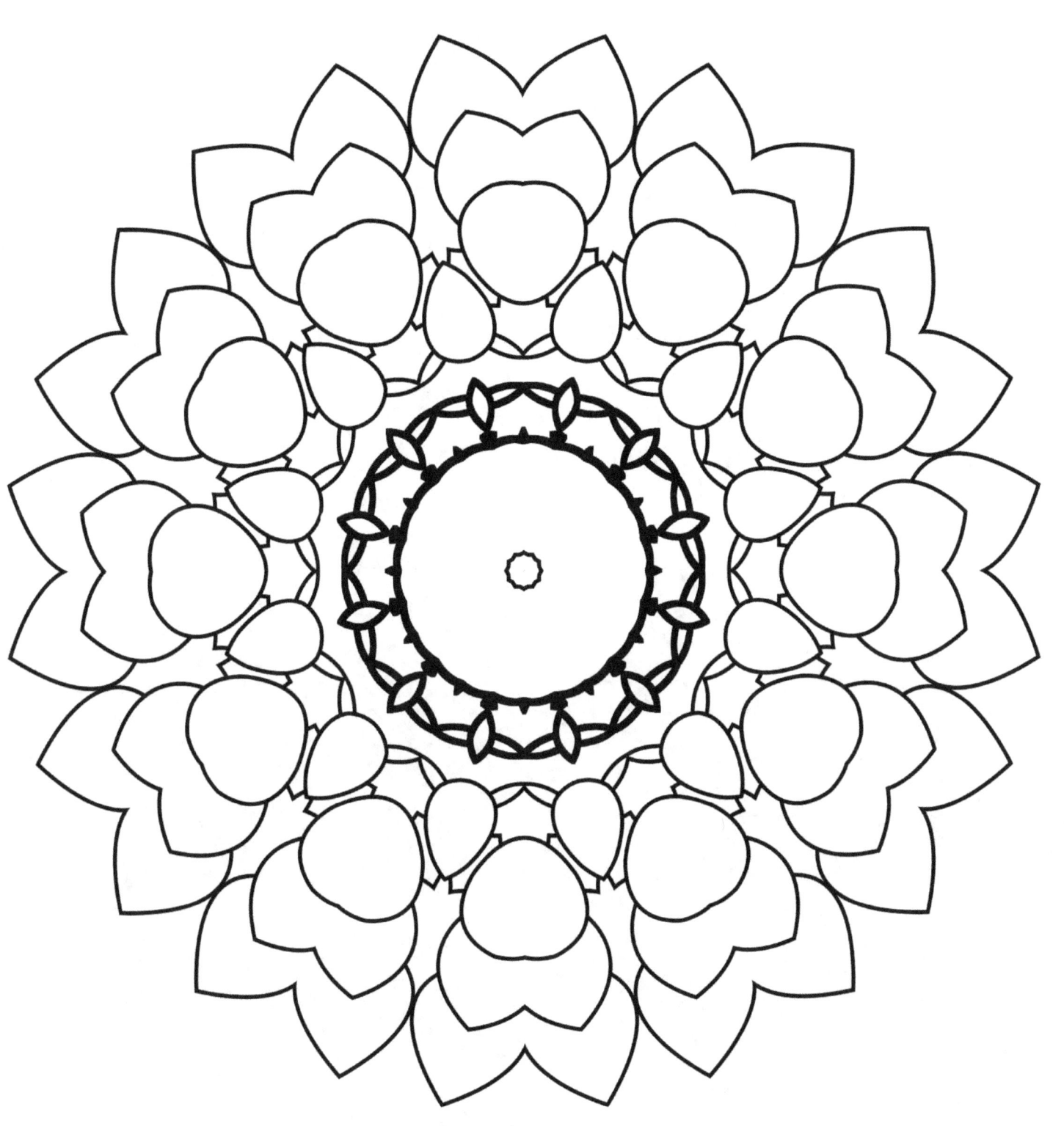

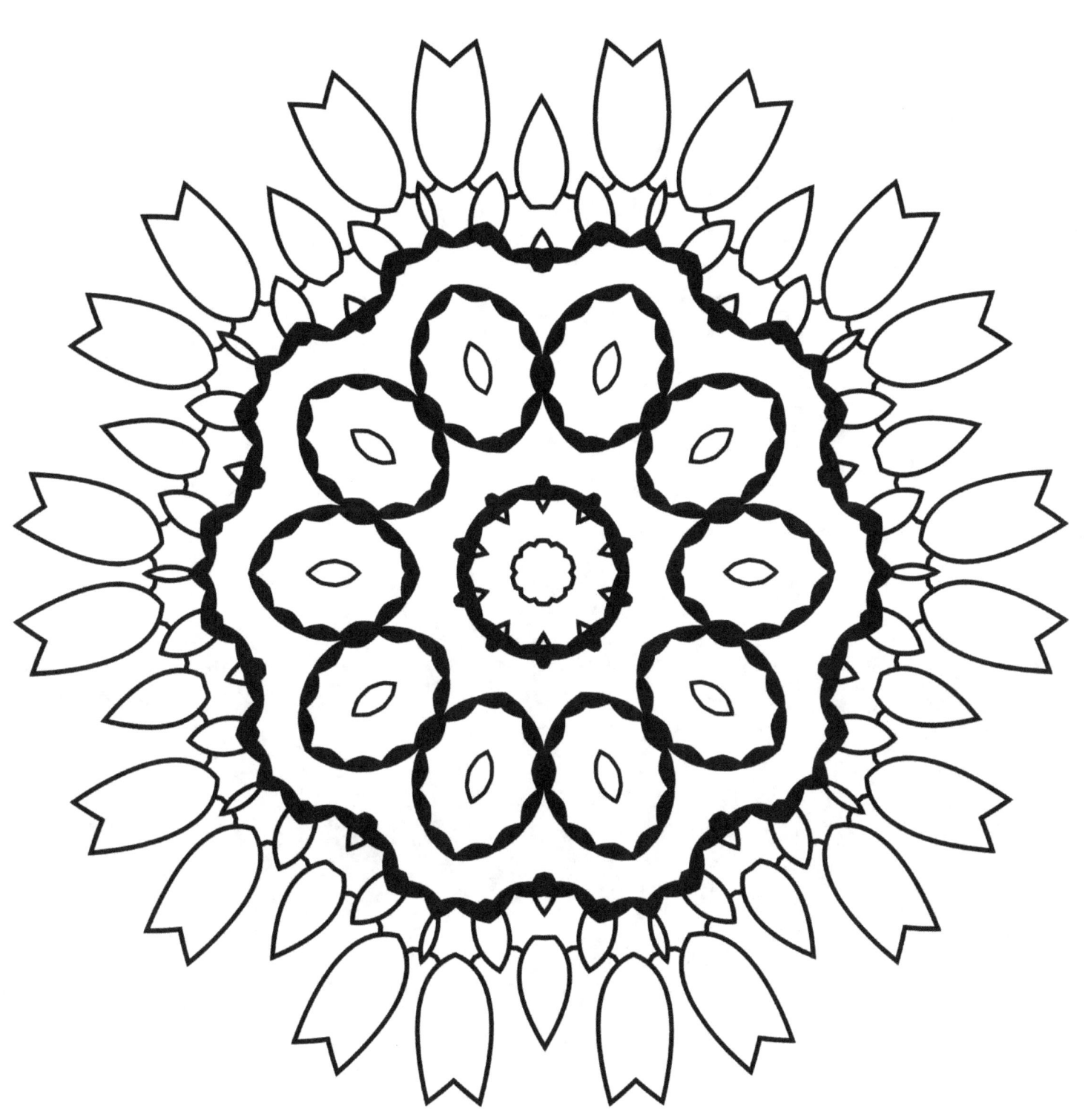

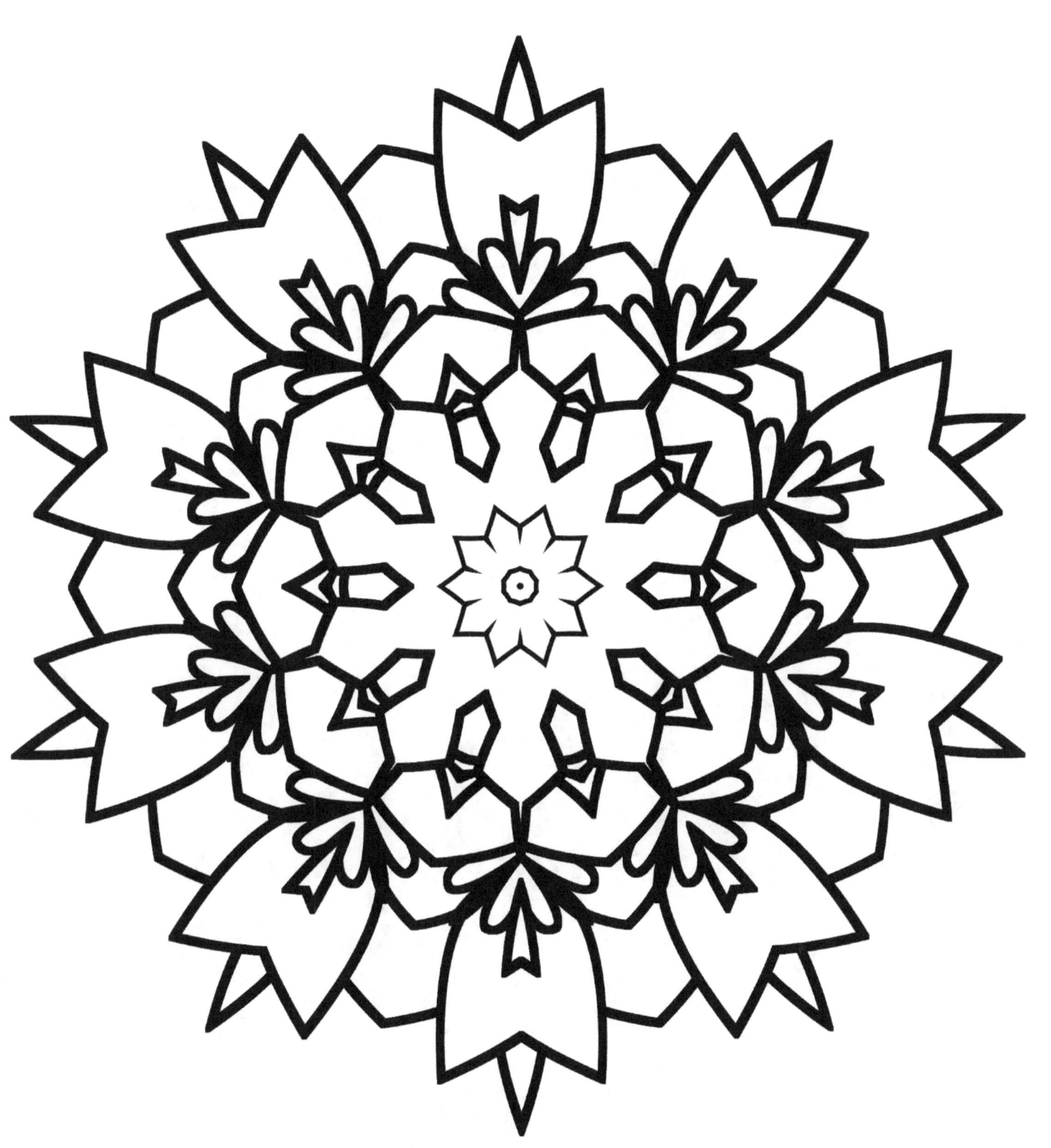

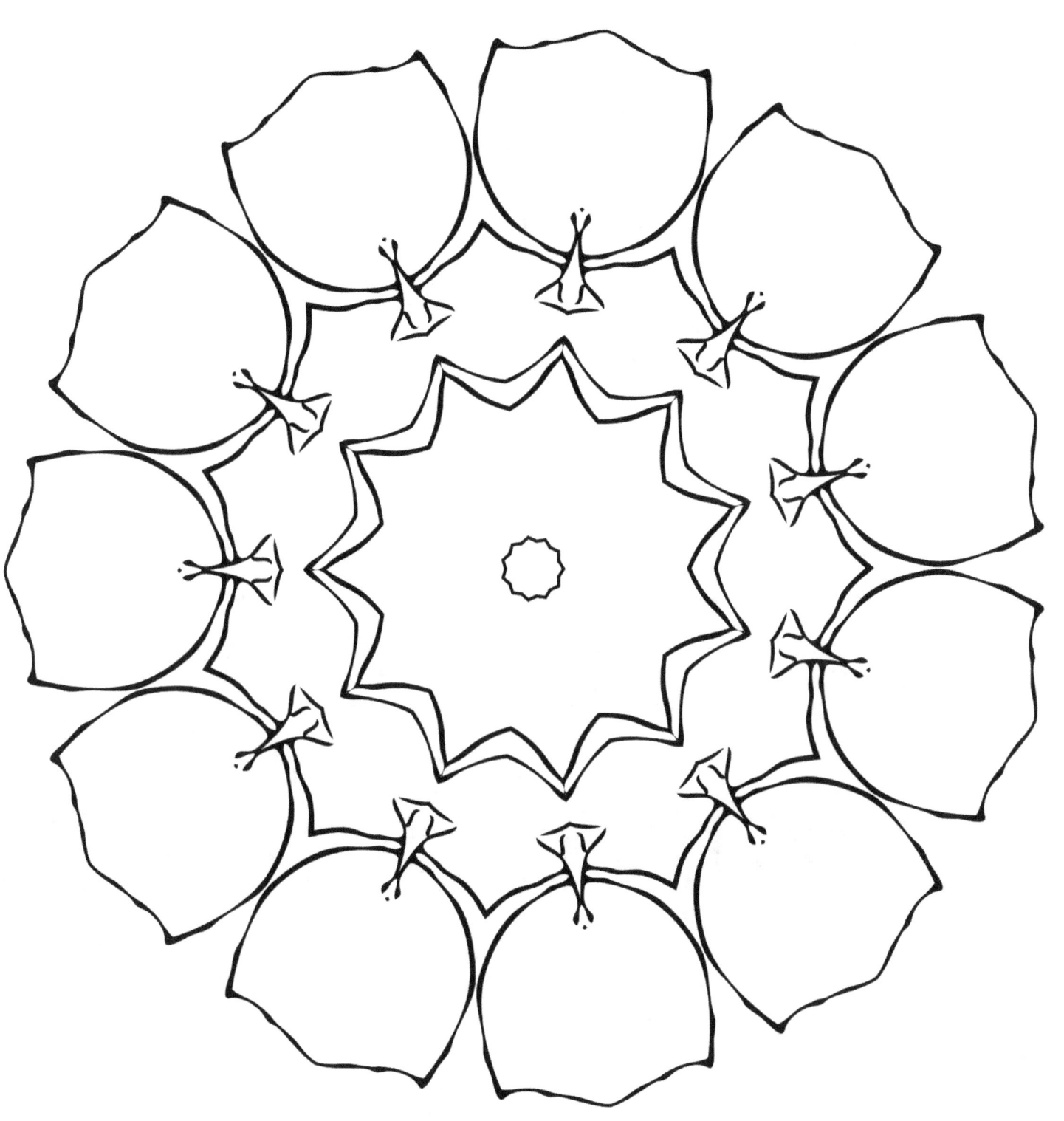

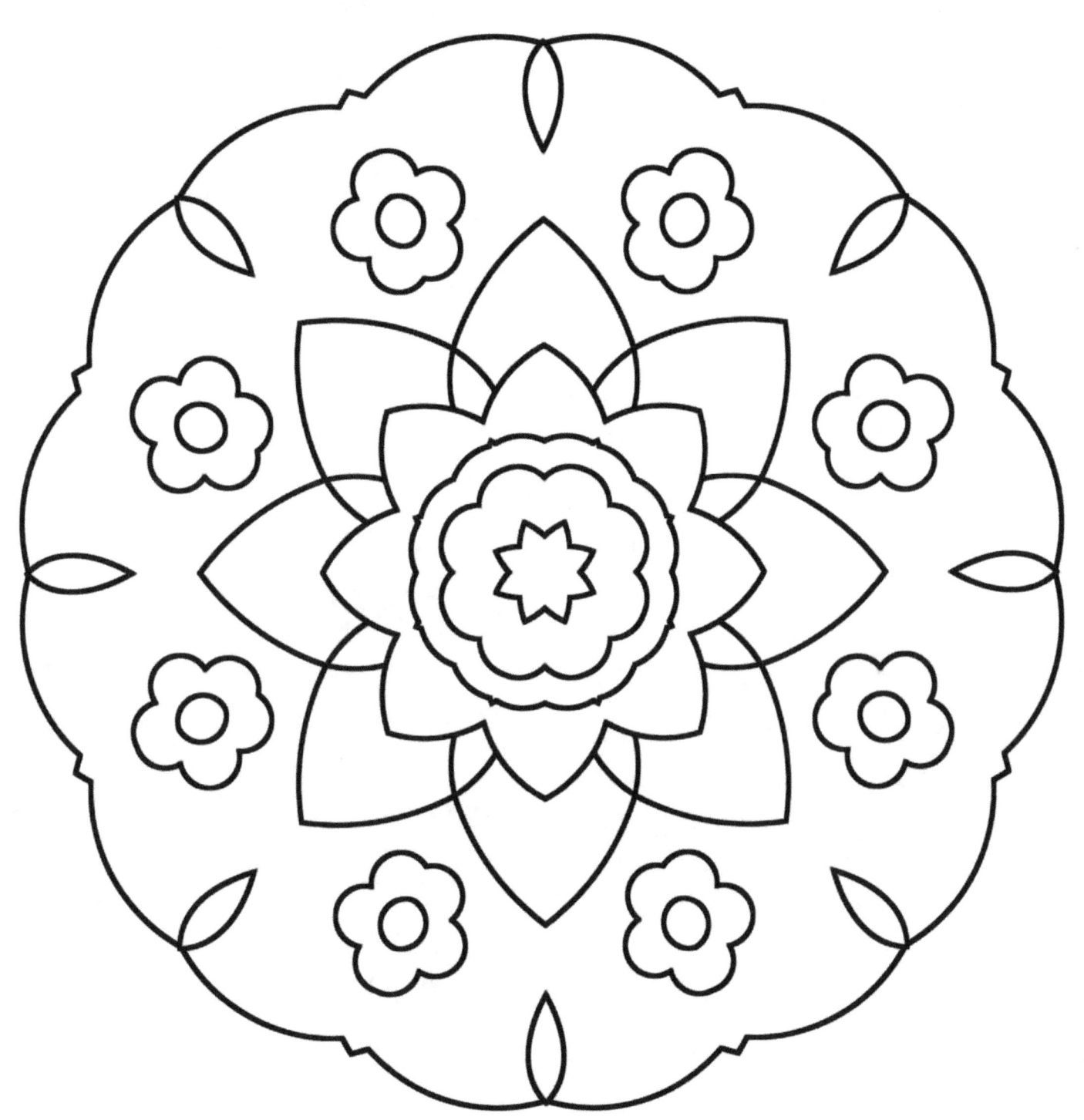

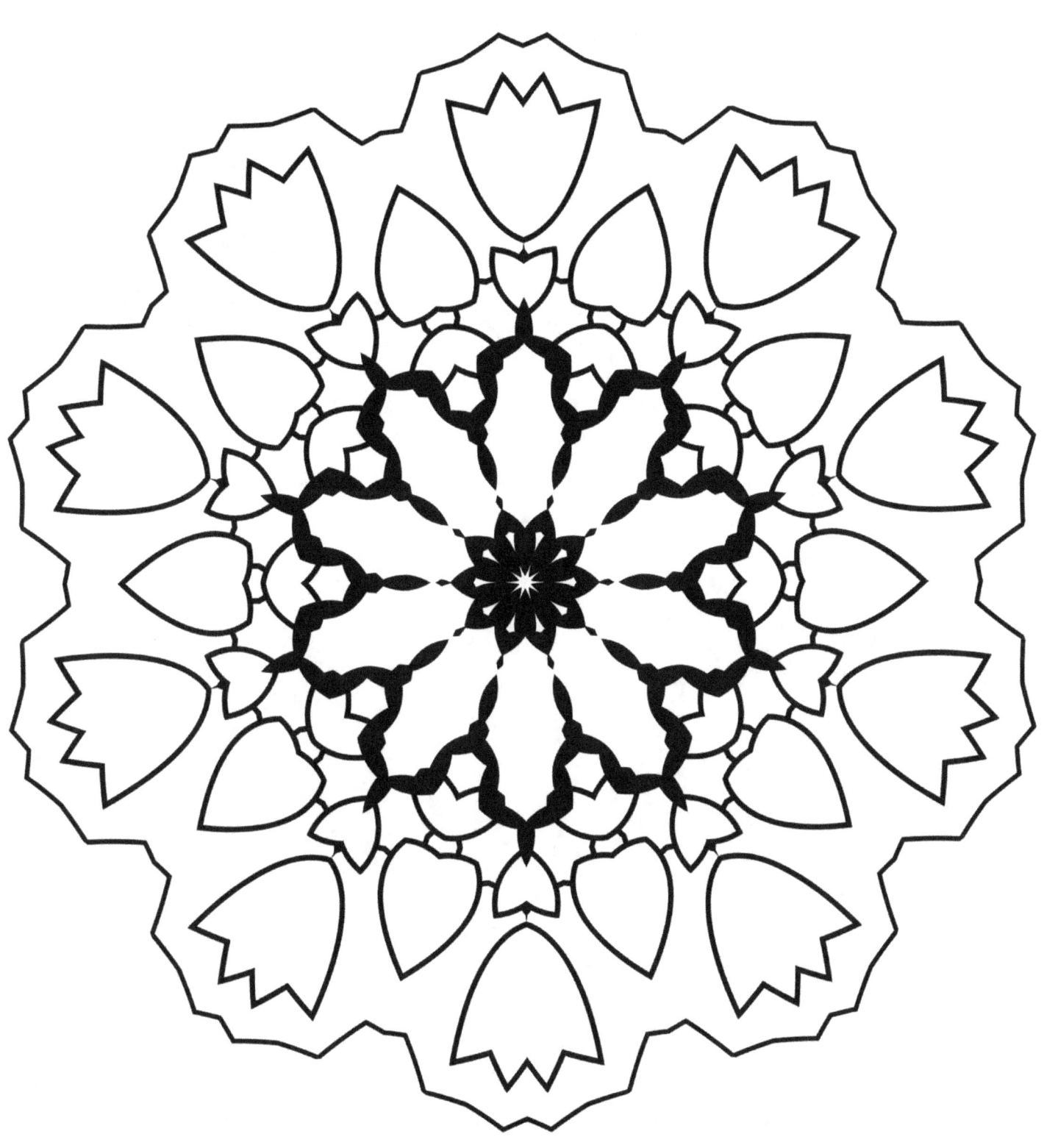

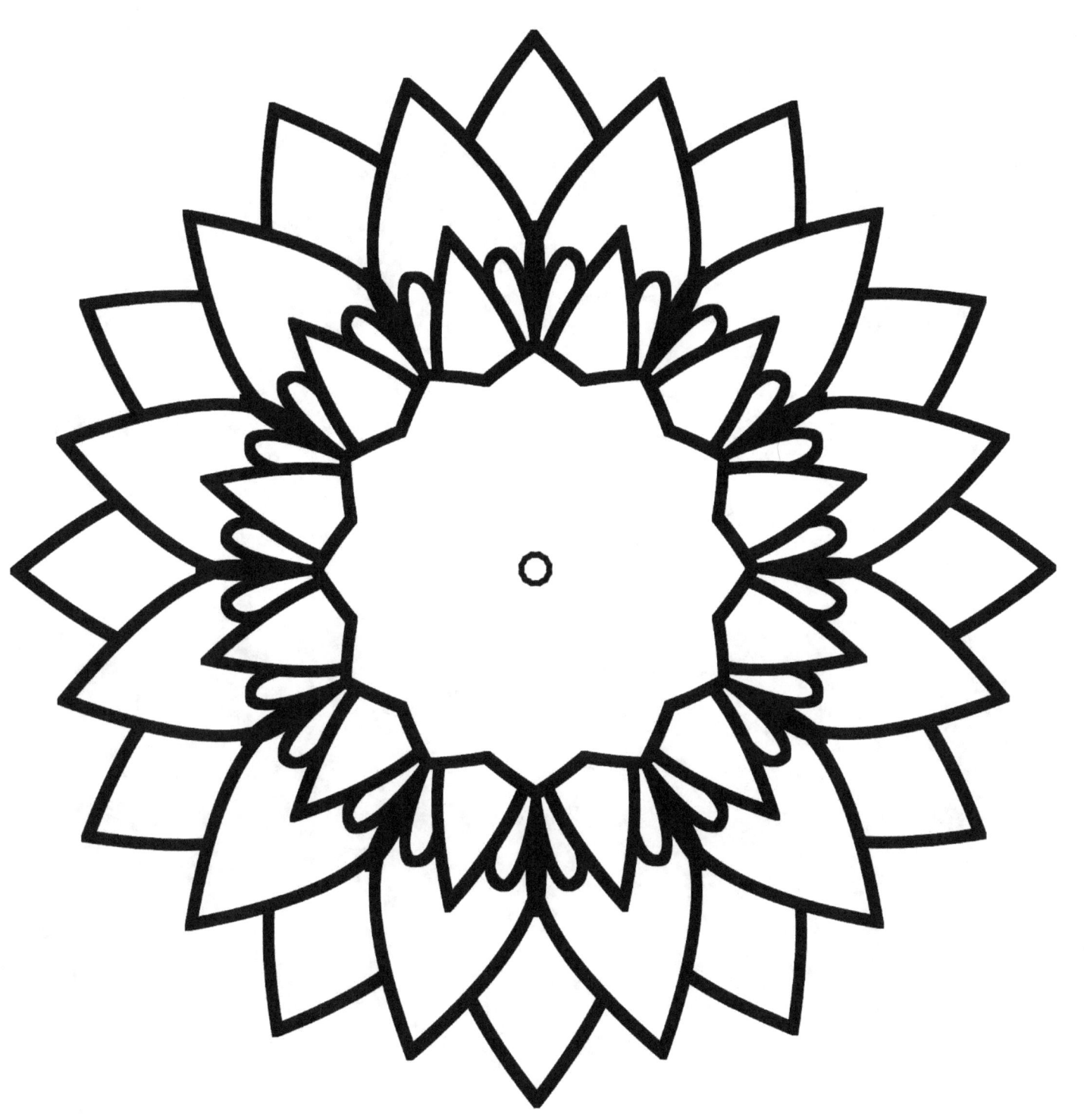

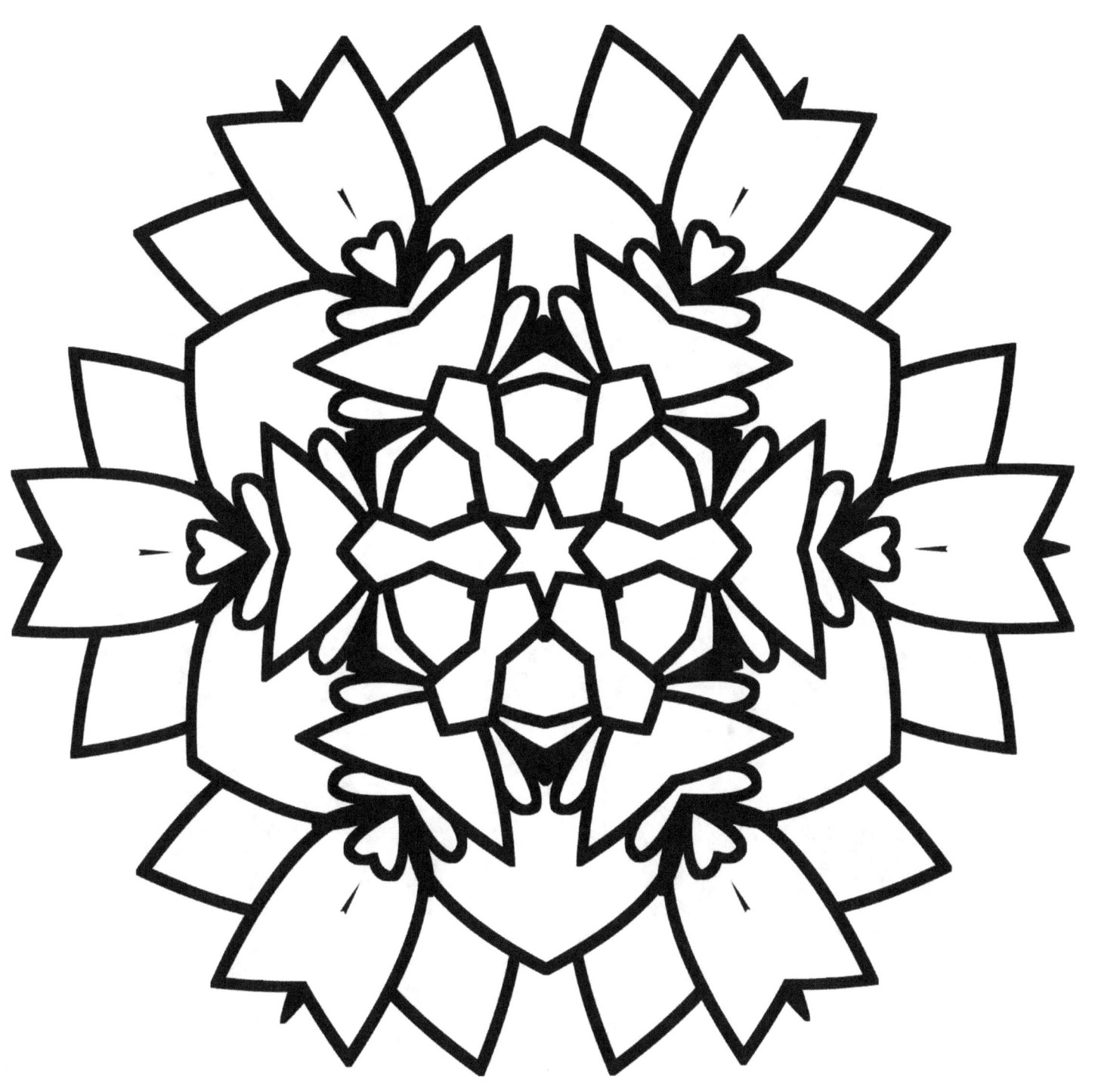

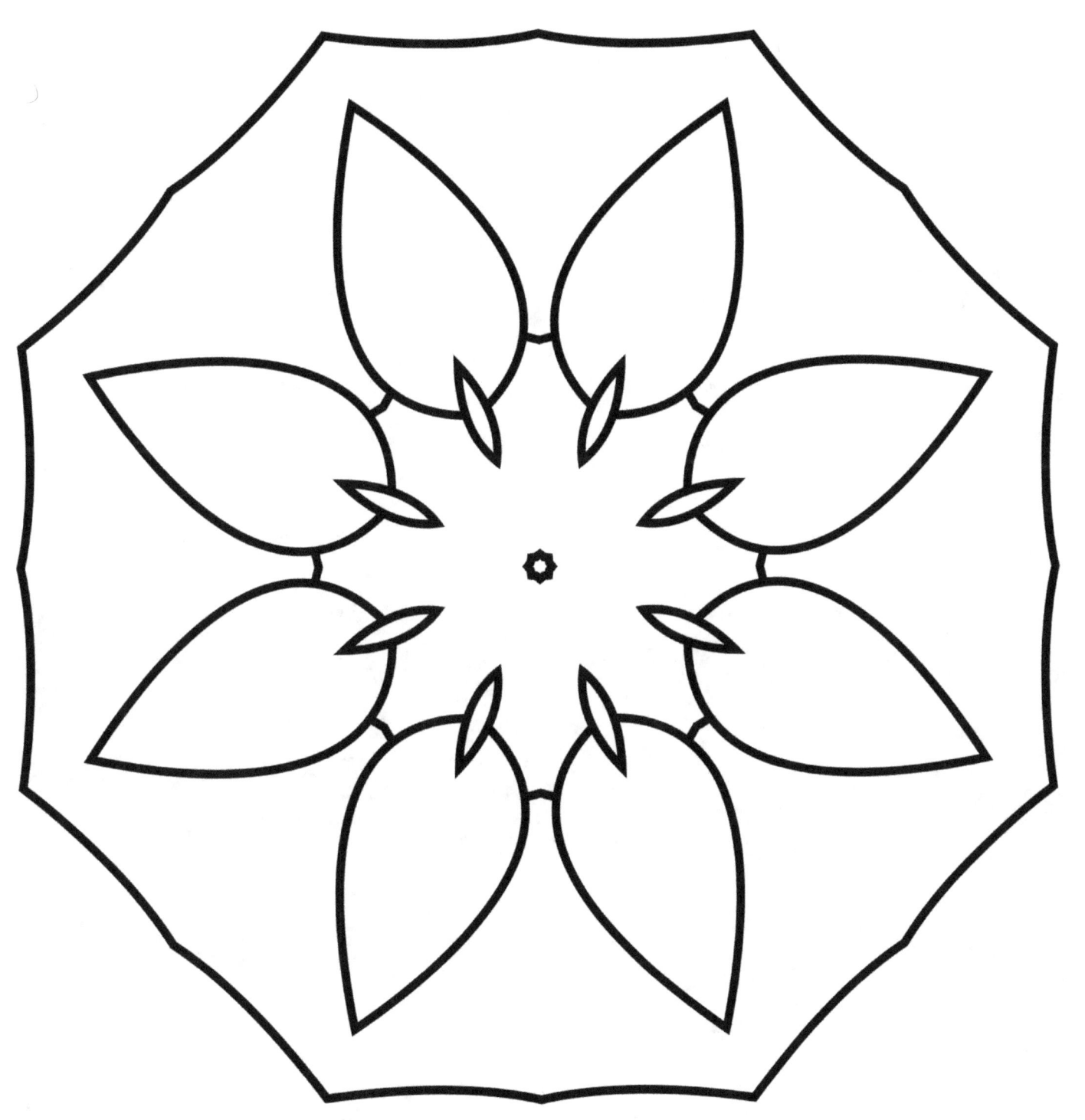

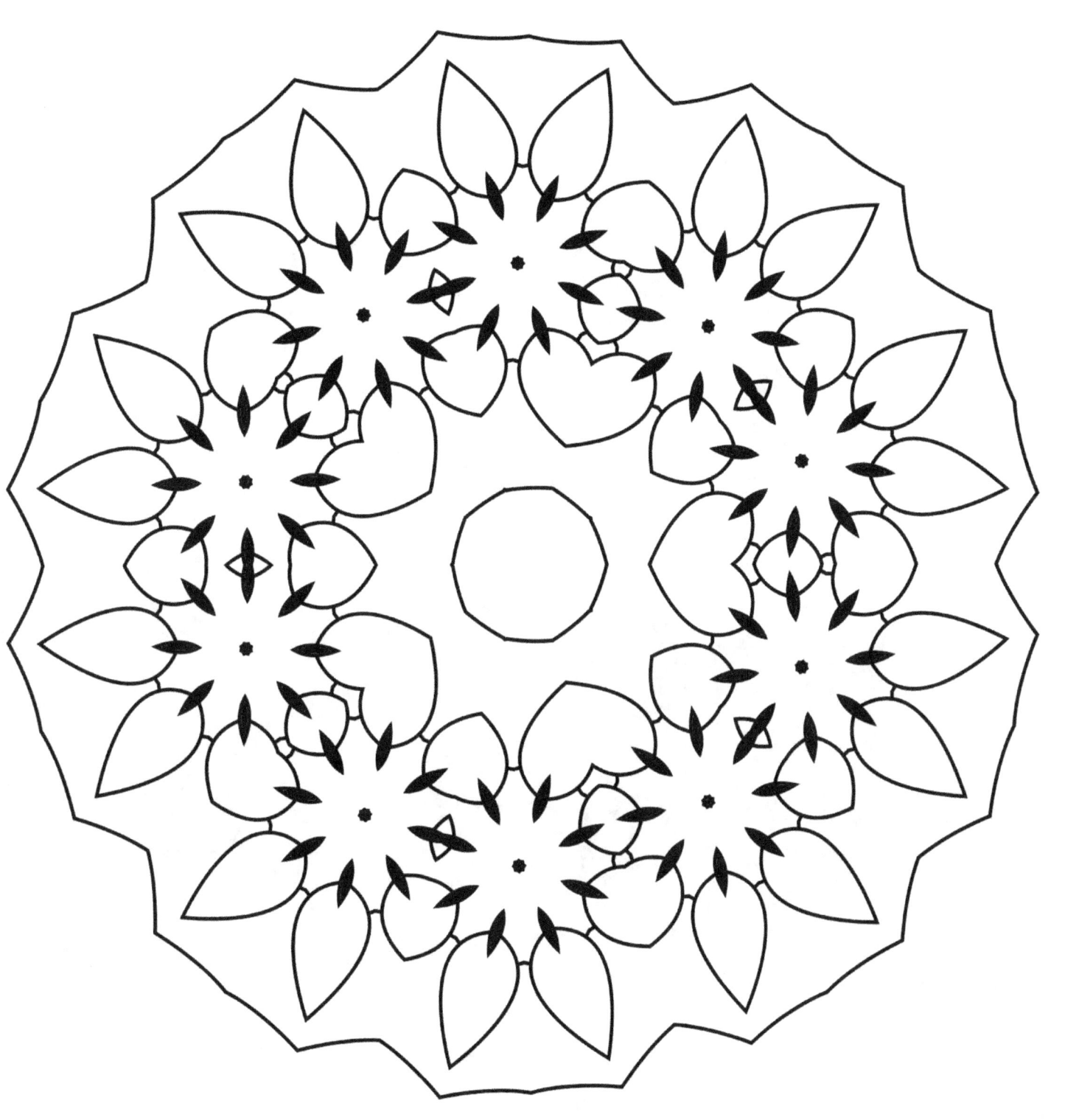

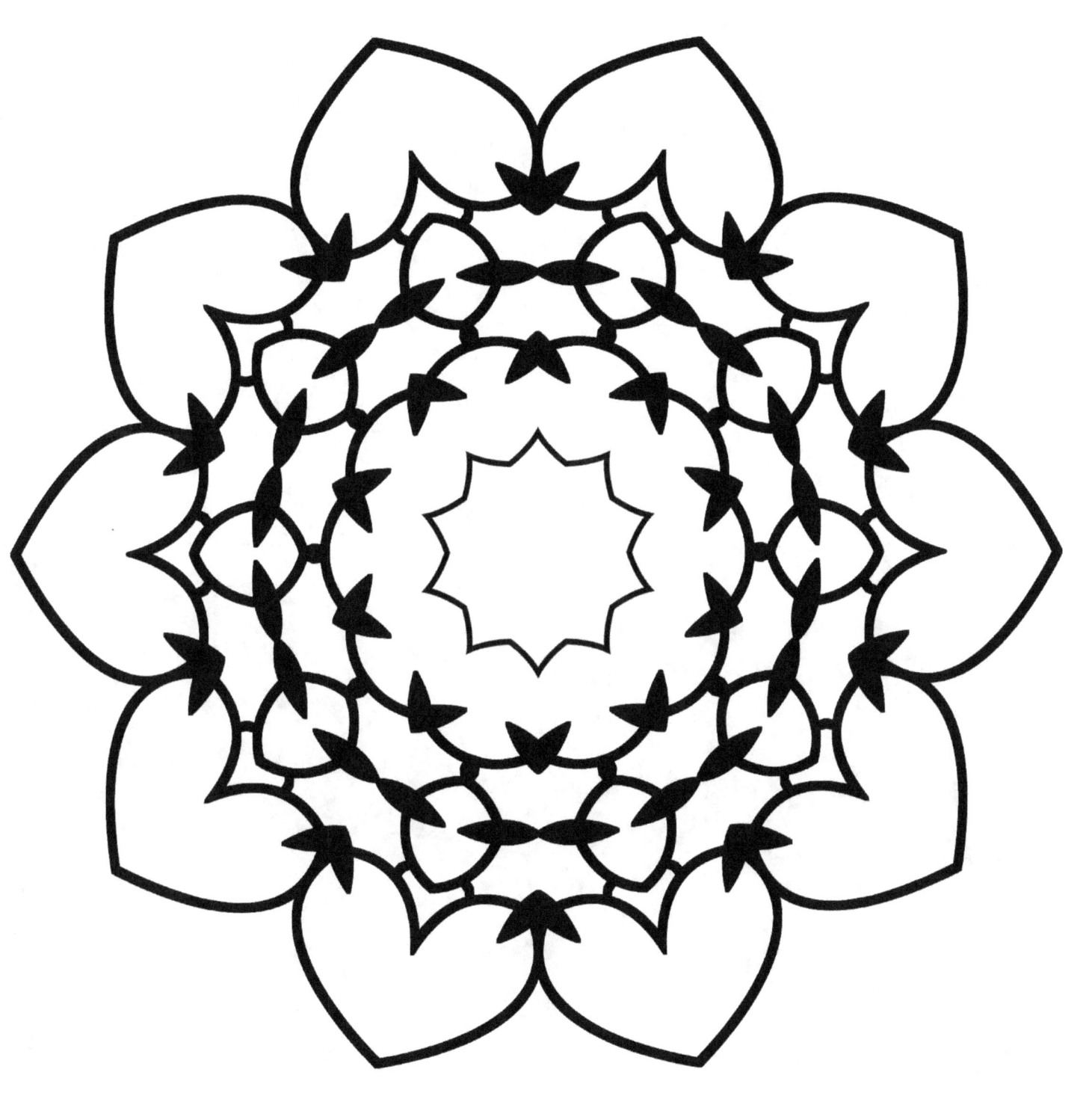

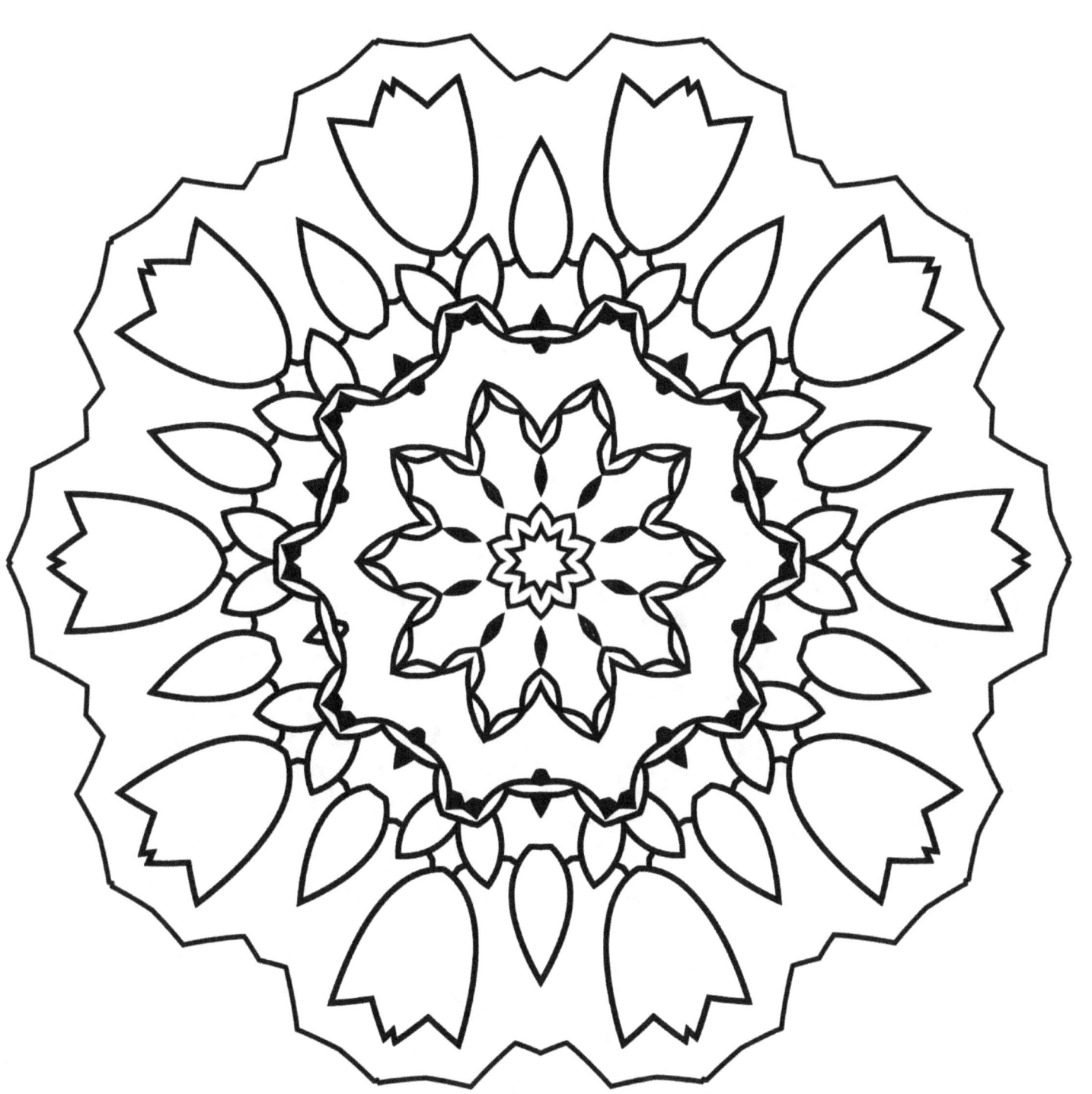

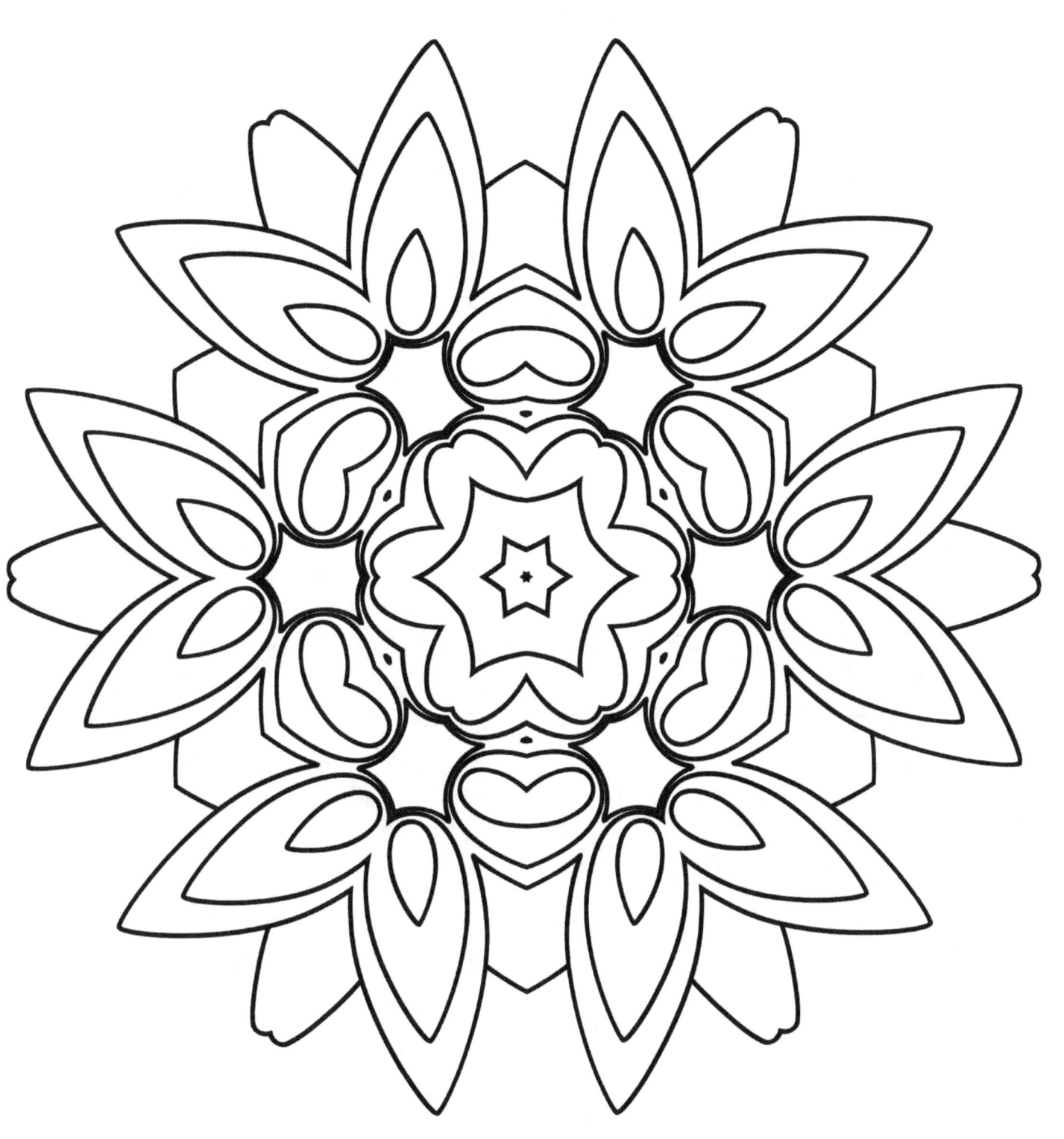

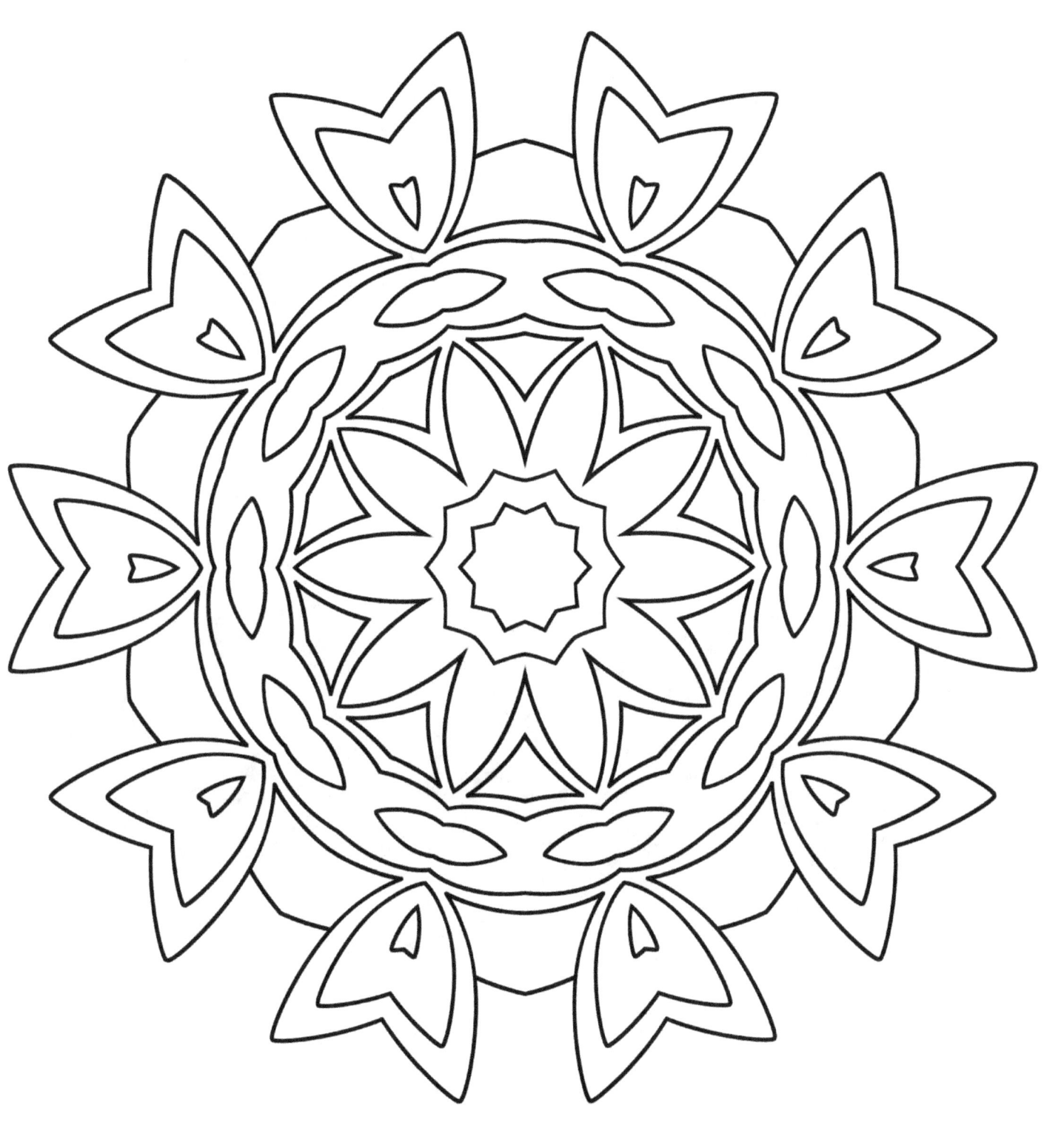

Easy Flower Mandalas
Adults Coloring Book

This coloring book for adults is my second book dedicated to beginners, seniors and individuals with low vision. I have included thirty-one delightful, one-sided illustrations to color as a relaxing and enjoyable pastime. You will find that these lovely floral mandalas are designed in bolder print and are not too detailed, making it easier for the artist to color.

Enjoy.

Lupita Romo

About Lupita Romo

Lupita Romo grew up in a family of artists. Both her parents inspired her to appreciate art and to follow her passion which eventually led her to complete a Bachelor Degree in Graphic Design and a University Diploma in Art. She likes bright colours and simple forms and loves art seen through the eyes of children. She enjoys sharing her passion by teaching art and the theory of colors to children and seniors alike.

Easy Flower Mandalas
Adults Coloring Book

ISBN-13: **978-1547177370**
ISBN-10: **1547177373**

You may also like:

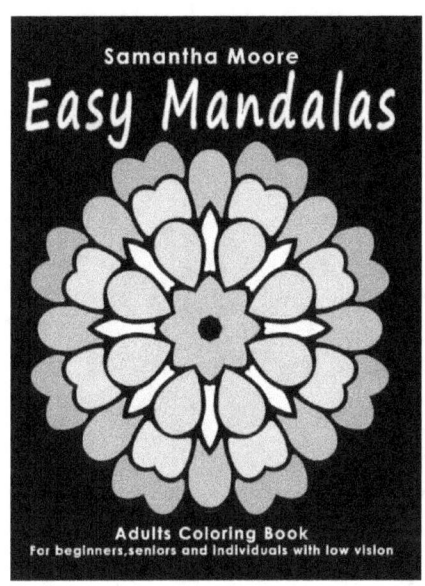

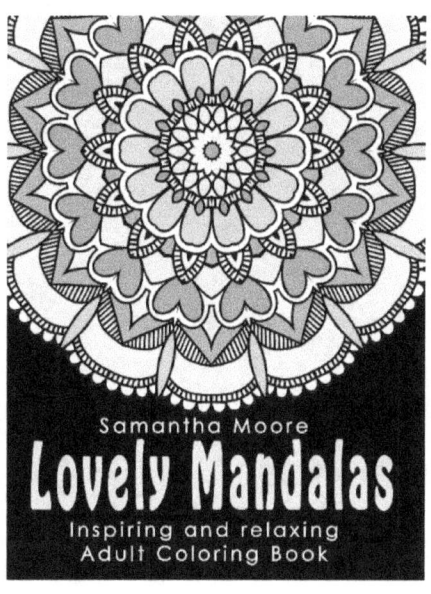

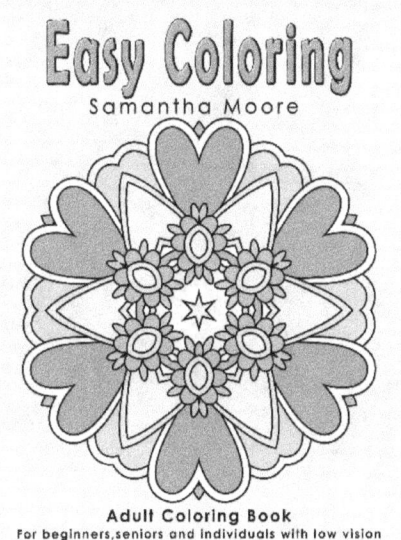

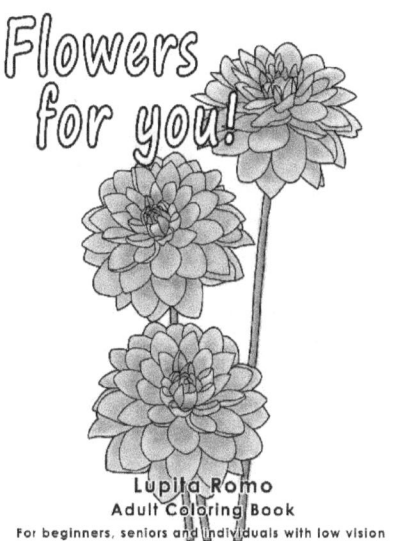

We would love to receive your comments. Please, find a moment to write a review on Amazon.

Thank you.